God called me to women's ministry forty-plus years ago, and for all of those years, discipleship has been at the center of my efforts. Seeking a discipleship strategy that works has been a struggle. I knew of the Gallatys' Replicate Ministries and had read about their D-Group strategy, so when God brought them to our church, I was ecstatic. Because of them, starting a D-Group with young women was the first thing I did when I retired. Being personally blessed doesn't even start to describe the experience I've had with these discipleship principles! All the details you need to disciple other women are right here in *Disciple Her*! And IT WORKS!

**Chris Adams,** retired women's ministry specialist at LifeWay Christian Resources and writer at *An Imperfect Woman in God's Perfect Plan* blog (chrisadams.blog)

While the Western church today is resource-rich and fat with Bible knowledge, too often that knowledge doesn't make its way into our lives. For all our knowledge, the truth is, our lives don't look all that different. My concern for the church is that we are becoming mere consumers of the Word instead of disciples whose lives are defined and directed by the Scriptures. Discipleship is the work of all believers—the catalyst for the church's growth into spiritual maturity *so that* we won't be "immature like children ... tossed and blown about by every wind of new teaching ... trick[ed] with lies so clever they sound like the truth" (Eph. 4:14). This means that each of us must take the call to make disciples seriously.

Kandi's book is a call to biblical discipleship. She shows that discipleship doesn't just happen by accident; we must be intentional. And "we" doesn't just mean a church program or the church staff or the "most spiritual" among us. It means all of us. Discipleship is the work that every Christian is called to do. Yet so many women are intimidated and aren't even sure how to start. This book demystifies discipleship and empowers women by providing concrete and practical tools they can implement. I highly recommend *Disciple Her* as a resource!

**Chrystie Cole,** women's discipleship advisor at Grace Church in Greenville, South Carolina, and author of Grace Church's Ezer discipleship studies, *Biblical Femininity, Redeeming Sexuality, Body Matters,* and *A Woman's Words*

Kandi Gallaty writes as a true practitioner of discipleship. She doesn't embody a program, but a discipleship lifestyle. If you are looking for a biblical and reproducible model to intentionally equip women in your life to be faithful Christ-followers, you have the right book in your hands.

**Kathy Litton,** director of planter spouse care at New American Mission Board and pastor's wife

Discipleship is deeply important, but so often I've held back from participating because of fear that I wasn't equipped and I wouldn't know where to start. In *Disciple Her*, Kandi offers a thoughtful resource that provided me the road map I needed. What a gift to have this resource!

**Lauren Green McAfee,** corporate ambassador for Hobby Lobby and coauthor of *Only One Life: How a Woman's Every Day Shapes an Eternal Legacy*

The multiplication process of discipleship is at the very core of vibrant Christianity. In her new book, *Disciple Her*, Kandi Gallaty gives women the necessary tools to engage in making disciples. True discipleship requires more than teaching a Bible study. As Kandi says, it is a lifestyle. Discipleship, by its very nature, leads to accountability and life sharing. Intimacy develops as you study God's Word together, pray together, and witness together.

If you have longed to be part of a discipleship group, but don't know where to start, this book is for you. It will give you the tools you need to say "yes" to Christ's command to make disciples, and it will help you let God use you to see lives transformed through the power of the gospel and His Word!

**Donna Gaines,** pastor's wife, founder and president of the board for ARISE2Read (a nonprofit that focuses on literacy in the inner city), radio show host for Memphis Women, and author of *A Daily Women's Devotional; Seated; Leaving Ordinary; There's Gotta Be More!; The Home Builders Bible Study; Fresh Brewed Faith Bible Study; Soul-Full Bible Study;* and *Choose Wisely, Live Fully*

In *Disciple Her,* you will be inspired, motivated, challenged, and equipped to fulfill your role as a discipler of other women. Kandi wonderfully reminds us that every Christian woman is called to do our part in sharing the Word, work, and wonder of God with everyone! This book will be a great resource for believing women everywhere.

**Jackie Green,** cofounder of the Museum of the Bible and coauthor of *This Dangerous Book* and *Only One Life: How a Woman's Every Day Shapes an Eternal Legacy*

# Disciple Her

# Disciple Her

*Using the Word, Work, & Wonder of God to Invest in Women*

## KANDI GALLATY

PUBLISHING GROUP

NASHVILLE, TENNESSEE

Published by B&H Publishing Group
Nashville, Tennessee

Dewey Decimal Classification: 248.5
Subject Heading: DISCIPLESHIP \ CHRISTIAN LIFE \
WITNESSING

2 3 4 5 6 7 8 • 23 22 21 20 19

To Robby,
my husband, my best friend,
my pastor and partner in ministry,
you are the love of my life and
I thank God for you daily.

# Acknowledgments

I would like to first thank Jesus, my Lord and Savior! Not only did You redeem me, but You also restored me. I could have never in a million years imagined writing a book. From start to finish, this has been a complete work of Yours!

I want to thank everyone at B&H and LifeWay for their desire to publish my work. I truly appreciate all of the men and women who have worked on this project. I am grateful for your thoughts, insights, edits, and encouragement.

Vivian Penuel, I can't thank you enough for proofreading this book. You were so kind to take on this project with such short notice.

Julie Woodruff, I love you, friend! You are a constant source of encouragement not only to me, but to all the women in our church! I am grateful to serve alongside you at Long Hollow as we make disciples.

I am grateful for each of the ladies whom I met with in discipleship groups over the years. I love you! The Lord has blessed me tremendously through every one of your relationships. I consider each of you a friend, and I have learned just as much from you as you think you have learned from me. Each group has been a learning and growing experience. The years we have spent together have forever marked my life.

Lori, Kim, Mollie, and Audrey, I cannot express what your friendships mean to me! I love each of you so much and deeply cherish our friendships. We have lived life together and discussed discipleship more times than I can count. You and your families are precious to me.

Stephanie, Barbie, Jen, Abby, Brooke, and Chris, thank you for serving alongside of me. You have prayed for me throughout this process, and I couldn't have done this without you. Being able to serve on staff together brings me so much joy! You are the best lead team wives ever.

To my in-laws and sister-in-law, I love you so much. As a family, you have been so good to me and have always accepted me as a daughter and a sister. You raised the most wonderful son. I see each of you in him. I am so proud to call you family.

To my parents, siblings, brother-in-law, nieces and nephews, thank you! I adore each of you, especially Baylen, Anabelle, Dominic, and Katherine. Being your Aunt K is the highlight of my life. I think about you every day. Mom and Dad, you raised me and shaped me into the woman I am today. I have learned so much from both of you. Mom, you truly are a Proverbs 31 woman.

Finally, to my boys, Robby, Rig, and Ryder, you have my heart. I cannot imagine life without you. Robby, being your wife has been the sweetest gift from the Lord. Rig and Ryder, you bring joy, purpose, and meaning to my life every day. The Lord teaches me through both of you all of the time. I am forever grateful to live for and serve our Lord together as a family.

# Contents

## Part 1: What Is Discipleship?

In this chapter, we will see that discipleship is a lifestyle—a pattern and way of life. In order to make disciples who make disciples who make disciples, you have to first be a disciple yourself. In order to lead others well, you have to lead yourself well. This chapter will look at the life of Jesus as a model for us to pattern our lives after.

In this section, we will learn that making disciples is from an overflow of what God is already doing in your life. You draw from three major sources when investing in the lives of others: God's Word, God's Work in your life, and God's Wonder, which is the Holy Spirit living inside of us.

## Part 2: Behind the Scenes of Discipleship

In this chapter, we will learn how to gauge success in a discipleship group with five criteria: Missional, Accountable, Reproducible, Communal, and Scriptural. Practical ways to follow through with each of these criteria will be included as well. We will also explore the difference between a D-Group and the other parts of church life we are used to, such as life groups/small groups/community groups and Sunday school.

Here we will learn about other characteristics to include in your group that will enhance your time together: Encouragement, Transparency, Confidentiality, Commitment, and Leadership.

In this chapter we will explore some of the effects of not making disciples, things like missing out on rich fellowship, having accountability, failing to realize your wealth in Christ, and enjoying the beauty of your walk with Christ. On top of those, the worst effect is that the only strategy given to the church by Jesus before His ascension is ignored. As a bonus, we will discuss how to avoid common frustrations.

After all the material we've covered, this chapter will finally answer the "Now what?" question. Based on all that was taught and suggested throughout the book, a final charge is given to go and disciple her.

## Appendices

## Notes 203

# Foreword

I am excited that discipleship is being talked about more today than ever before; however, I'm concerned about the future. Many are slapping the "discipleship" label on everything from hangouts, to Bible studies, to pizza socials, to Sunday night training classes. When we fail to define what we are talking about, the term can be applied to anything and everything, causing it to lose its meaning. While things like hangouts and Bible studies may contain elements of discipleship, it's so much more than that. Discipleship is the course of your life.

In addition to defining the terms of what discipleship is and looks like, we must chart a pathway for spiritual growth. Like you, I've read books on the philosophy of discipleship, the theology of discipleship, and the reasons for making disciples. However, I walked away wanting to know how to implement what I learned. When Jesus commanded His disciples in the Great Commission to "Go, therefore, and make disciples" (Matt. 28:19), it was not a theoretical concept. Using His own everyday life, He spent three years modeling what He expected them to do. Good leaders do this with those around them. They model what they expect others to do.

While plenty of men have written many books about making disciples (I've written some), resources for women written by a woman on how to actually disciple other women are scarce. This is why I'm so excited Kandi has written this book. She has defined what discipleship is and outlined a pathway for investing in other women.

Anyone who has ever met Kandi knows that she lives and breathes discipleship. Some might think she got that passion from me, but she possessed a desire to invest in women before we met. When we started dating, she was already pouring her life into a group of ladies weekly through Bible study, accountability, and encouragement. Most of our conversations at that time were about how we could grow spiritually in our walk with Christ by discipling others. We shared what we were studying in the Bible, what Scriptures we were memorizing, and what books we were reading.

God has called us both to ministry. I wouldn't be the person I am today without Kandi. No one has shaped my life more than she has. Her faithfulness in reading the Word daily has motivated me to do the same. It's a rare morning that I wake up and don't find her on the couch spending time in the Bible. Her commitment to Scripture memory has inspired me to hide it in my own heart. She embodies every principle in this book.

If you're a Christian woman, I'd encourage you to form a group of women in a D-Group setting (three to six people) and read this book together. Talk about the principles you've learned and develop a strategy for implementing them in your life. Every woman will benefit from this book.

Robby Gallaty

# Introduction

If you want to know what kind of benefit discipleship can have in your life, I'd suggest taking a spin class.

We have a home gym and an elliptical machine in our house, which are great. I love going on walks, which is fine too. But what I love the most are the two or three times a week I go to the gym and ride for half an hour alongside others who are pushing hard and accomplishing the goals they've set for themselves. In this class, we sit on specialized bikes that allow you to set up a personal profile each time you get on the bike. You type in your age, weight, whether you are male or female, and how many hours of cardio you do each week on average, and then it gives you a number—called your Functional Threshold Watt rate, or FTW—based on all of that information.

The bike also has a monitor with five colors on it: white, blue, green, yellow, and red. If you are pedaling and the white light is lit, you are pedaling just barely over a standstill. If the light is blue, you're pedaling a bit harder, green is harder than that, yellow is pushing yourself, and red is an all-out sprint. Green is your fat-burning zone and is where you should spend most of your time during the class. The

FTW you input before beginning tells your bike how much resistance to give you. The higher your FTW, the more difficult it will be to stay in each zone.

At the end of each class, your bike will tell you how much time you spent in each zone. Ideally, you spent most of your time at a steady green pace. You can have some yellow—it's okay to push hard for a little while, so long as you are not doing it at the expense of being able to complete the race. If you try to sprint for too long, you won't finish. On the flip side, if you spend too much time in white, you won't get anything out of the class.

This spin class is discipleship in miniature. When we get saved, we are on fire for God—we're in the all-out, anaerobic red sprint of our exercise bike. We're firing on all cylinders, telling everyone we've ever known about Jesus. No one could shut us up if they tried.

Frankly, nobody lives in that state forever. We eventually taper off and become more even-keeled. We may experience a high point and live for a while in "yellow"—we might be passionate about certain ministries or different opportunities that come up and ignite a more sustainable, but not long-lasting, fire in our hearts. Some of us find that we dip into the white and blue zones—we're coasting along, not pushing or trying. You're just in this Christianity thing for the ride. You love Jesus, but there's not a lot of fruit being born.

But green is that steady zone. The good zone. Living in the "green" in your Christian life means you're showing constant, steady growth. You're building endurance without breaking yourself down. You're in it for the long haul, not just the short sprint.

Discipleship puts you in the spiritual green zone. It means you're coming alongside other women and spending time in the Word of God, memorizing it, journaling, holding one another accountable, and praying together. Sharing your faith, fasting, and worship are other spiritual disciplines that you can do individually but are also highly effective when practiced in community. Discipleship is not a program, it's a way of life. It's how we maintain a healthy, balanced spiritual journey. In his book *Spiritual Disciplines for the Christian Life*, Don Whitney says, "Now the goal of practicing any given discipline is not about doing as much as it is about being; being like Jesus, being with Jesus."[1] We discipline ourselves and practice these activities to be more like Him.

Part of what makes spin class so awesome is not only the room full of others riding and pushing themselves like you are, but the accountability of the colored lights on the bike. There is no faking a color when the instructor tells you to move to green or hold yellow. It is plain for all to see. The same is true in a discipleship group. You are surrounded by a small group of trusted ladies, and you can't fake it with them. You are riding and pushing together as a unit with the same goal: to remain steady on your ride as the Lord works in your life. Each lady can be and will be in different seasons as they journey together, and that's fine. Discipleship isn't only for the "spiritual elite." It doesn't matter if you are in a fertile season or a dry one. You will learn from one another, which is the beauty of the process.

The most important spiritual discipline in your life is the daily reading of God's Word. This is a strong statement, I know, but it is one I believe with every fiber of my being. Spending time in Scripture is of the utmost importance because our lives ebb and flow in and out of different seasons. It never stays the same for very long. Sometimes those seasons will be times of joy and celebration; sometimes they will be filled with suffering and difficulty. Nevertheless, the Word of God remains the same. In a world of flux, it is our one constant for direction, guidance, encouragement, motivation, inspiration, confrontation, conviction, and remembrance.

How will you learn to navigate your upcoming wedding and marriage? The birth of your child? How about raising your kids, dealing with a miscarriage, a diagnosis of a special-needs child, the loss of your home due to flooding or fire? What about when your coworkers or fellow students snub you, gossip about you, or talk negatively? What about when you lose a parent, spouse, friend, or even a community when you have to move away? How about when God calls you to step out in faith and do something new or go somewhere you have never been? When anything at all happens to you, how will you know how to respond?

In all these situations and more, God speaks to us through His Word as He does the work in our lives. Coming alongside others to read and discuss the Word of God is the crux of discipleship, and gives us the ability to navigate life's changing terrain with the right compass.

Perhaps you're asking, "Okay, I agree, but what does discipleship look like? Is it just another church program I have to sign up for?" Or maybe you're saying, "I'm in, but I have no idea where to start."

In this book, I will draw on the way that Jesus made disciples and share my own experience in disciple-making in order to show you that it *is* something you can do, starting today. Drawing from the experiences God has given my husband and me, I will share what is effective, what is ineffective, and what makes the discipleship process run smoothly.

Above everything else I say in this book, I most importantly hope to explore with you what it means to take Jesus' final command—to make disciples of all nations—seriously. And that only happens in a discipling community.

Community is what we were created for, both with others and with God. Let us learn about community in the context of a discipleship group, and figure out how it will change your life and the lives of others for years and years to come.

PART 1

# What Is Discipleship?

# The DNA of a Disciple-Maker

I was not the first of my friends to have children, but that didn't stop me from having opinions about them. Many times, I'd be sitting in their living rooms or out with them at lunch and the kids would start acting out or becoming disrespectful. Sooner or later, the kids would start throwing fits for not getting their way. And I'd sit there, imagining all the ways the mom should just get those kids under control!

You know what I'm talking about. We've all been there. We see a little toddler throwing a tantrum for not getting his way or being loudly disrespectful. You may see them throwing themselves down in the toy aisle or refusing to obey simple instructions. I remember thinking on more than one occasion, *My child will never act that way.*

Well, the Lord has a sense of humor, doesn't He?

I was soon blessed with two rambunctious boys and found myself eating my words (even if I just kept them to myself). My sons are absolute blessings, but they keep me on my toes—and sometimes at my wit's end. I learned quickly that my opinions about parenting weren't worth much until I became a parent myself. I needed to be in that role and position before I acted like I knew what I was doing. And believe me, I get a lot of hands-on training.

I was recently at the store with them as they provided the entertainment for the long line of customers waiting to check out. When it was finally our turn, the sweet cashier said with a smile on her face, "You certainly have your hands full!" And she is right. There is nothing like being a mom of boys very close in age. I happened to learn this in parenting, but the same is true for anything really—like the people with no real creative training or experience, yet think they are a professional photographer simply because they have an iPhone and Instagram. Or the people who tell their kid's teacher what to do when they've never worked a day in the educational field. Or the people who ramble to their doctor about what Google said, though there's obviously only one person in the room who actually went to medical school. It's funny how we, in one way or another, can have opinions on things of which we have never had an active role in.

That is exactly how discipleship works. You have to be a disciple yourself before you make disciples. You must *be* before you can *do*. Don't be scared by that sentence—being a disciple simply means being a lifelong learner. It is a lifestyle of leading yourself so that you can lead others. When God called us to Himself, it was a call to discipleship. It was a calling to follow after Him.

## Abide in the Word

One of my goals when I am meeting with ladies in my discipleship groups (called D-Groups from here on out) is to help them develop spiritual disciplines that will last a lifetime. The Bible says in John 8:31–32, "Then Jesus said to the Jews who had believed him, 'If you continue in my word, you really are my disciples. You will know the truth, and the truth will set you free.'" The disciple-maker's goal is to make disciples who are passionate about God's truth.

Jesus said something interesting in those verses. He used the word *continue*, which means to remain, abide, to keep being present. It is an ongoing relationship, not a momentary one. By *continuing*, you will know the truth and that truth will set you free. It will deliver you and liberate you. I like to rhyme when I can, so I tell women I disciple, "In order to survive and thrive you need to abide." We need to be grounded and rooted in the Word of God.

While some new converts have an insatiable and immediate appetite for Scripture, some don't. Not everyone magically has a love and desire for the Word after getting saved. It doesn't even automatically come when you get into a discipleship relationship. It's like with any other relationship when you love someone: the more you know them, the more you love them and want to spend time with them.

When Robby and I were dating, we spent a summer apart because he was a camp pastor in Glorieta, New Mexico. He was gone for more than two months. We would talk every day on the phone for as long as we could, and we were always writing emails to each other. Robby would email me the sweetest letters and poems; I would save them and read them over and over. Eventually I printed them out and laminated them. I love to go back and read his letters to me. I keep them in our keepsake box so that we have them to show our boys one day.

I not only have a keepsake box for Robby and me, but for both of our boys too. All of the items near and dear to our hearts go in those boxes so we can pull them out from time to time and reminisce. That is how most keepsake boxes work: we put them on a shelf in the closet and pull them out only when we feel like it.

The sad truth is most of us treat the Bible the same way. We consider it precious but not a priority. We want to have one and keep it safe but we don't want to saturate ourselves with it. It sits collecting dust even though we are called to *continue* in Jesus' Word. We are to steep ourselves in it, sit and soak in it. Too often we are content just dipping our toes in either for the sake of getting a sweet pick-me-up when we need it, or simply for the sake of having done it.

Even now, the more I spend time with my husband, the more I love and appreciate him. We have been married for fourteen years and I love him more now than I ever could have on our wedding day. That is because I know him so much better than I did then. We have spent time together and we have grown in our relationship.

The Bible works the same way. I loved reading Robby's words to me, but they weren't what gave me life. While words from the man I love could remind me how he felt and help strengthen my relationship with him, only God's words have the power to change and sustain me! The more you spend time with God reading and applying His word, the more you love, respect, and admire it. It becomes your life's consuming passion.

## Cherish the Word

Sometimes hearing other people's passion for God's Word helps inspire our own. One person—William McPherson—had a commitment to Scripture that was remarkable. He was a Scottish quarry worker who came to America in 1893 and settled outside of Denver. A hard worker, William eventually earned the spot of quarry superintendent. Though he had a number of admirable traits, he tended to be a bit impatient at times.

One day his impatience got the best of him and he grabbed a live stick of dynamite. It exploded while he was hovered over it. They were hours away from a doctor, but thanks to the efforts of his coworkers, he didn't die. Unfortunately, though, the accident left him with no hands, little feeling in his face, and no eyesight. From that moment on, he was blind.

Up to this point in his life he had lived for himself, reckless and free. Now, he was entirely dependent on others to help him get by. On several occasions before, others had tried to share Christ with him; now, due to his accident, he was in a place to listen.

He gave his heart to the Lord in the coming months but was not satisfied by simply having someone read Scripture to him. He longed for the ability to read it for himself.

His injury was taxing to those around him, though—emotionally, physically, and financially. Eventually, his family found themselves unable to take care of him so he entered a home in Illinois for the aged and disabled. Day in and day out he lived in darkness and solitude. He lived out the repetitive mornings, the same-song afternoons, and the identical evenings, armed with little more than his new-found hope in Christ. It was desperately lonely, and he had little hope that anything about his life would change until he died.

At the nearby school, lecturers would come and speak about various topics that the people in the home were facing. One day he learned of a young blind girl who had learned Braille and was able to read her Bible with her fingertips. William couldn't do this because the explosion had taken his hands. Over time, this young girl lost the feeling in her own hands and was distraught. She brought the Bible to her lips one day to kiss it goodbye, and to her amazement, felt something. She discovered that she could feel the raised letters with her lips!

The story of this young girl had William pondering whether there was hope for him. He had lived in blackness for five years when God sent a blind girl named Anna Johnson to the home to work with some of the blind patients. Working with William proved to be frustrating, though: he had no hands, so conventional reading wouldn't work. He had no feeling in his face, so the technique the little girl had adopted wouldn't work either, although they tried many times. One day William asked Anna when she was about to go home for the day, if she could leave with him one of the little cards they had been practicing with.

He kept trying to feel the little raised bumps with different parts of his body, when he realized he had not prayed and asked God for help. So he earnestly begged God for help. The next time he raised the card to his lips, his tongue slipped out and brushed the paper. To his astonishment, he could feel the raised letters with his tongue! He couldn't wait for Anna to come back so he could tell her.

With Anna's help, William learned how to read braille with his tongue. In the sixty-five years that followed, and after much bleeding and soreness, William McPherson read the entire Bible four times with his tongue.[2]

I am absolutely blown away by this man. His example leaves those of us who can see with no excuse. God forbid we die and stand next to William in heaven, and we can't say that we have read the Bible once with all parts of our body functioning properly. That would be a true tragedy.

The year I heard this, I happened to be in the middle of reading the Bible in its entirety for the first time. At the end of the year, on December 31, I went to Robby in tears and told him, "If I die and stand next to William, I can say I have one under my belt. He would have four and I would have one."

Then the next year came and on December 31, I went to Robby and I said, "If I die and stand next to William, he will have four and I have two." It became a sort of benchmark for me, a small way to measure how devoted I was to spending time in God's Word. I wasn't rushing through, I wasn't using Bible reading as a measure of my relationship, but rather as something of a barometer for my passion. By the end of the third year I could tell William if I saw him in heaven that I had read God's Word three times through. Though that was a feat by itself, something even more remarkable had happened: I had cultivated a passion for the Word of God.

As the years have gone on, I have learned that I don't have to read the Bible in its entirety every year. It's not about the quantity of Scripture we read, but the quality time spent in it. As my focus shifted from reading large quantities of Scripture to smaller, I've noticed that I now read "less" in order to digest more. But this is all just a part of my journey. If you have never read the Bible through, I cannot stress enough how enriching of an experience it is. You get a full view of the work that God has done in His people and see how His plan fits together perfectly—and continues to this day. If you've never read it through, it is never too late to begin.

The *Chicago Tribune* published an article about William on April 27, 1913. In it, William commented that he believed that he was uplifted spiritually by being struck down physically. Though his vision was dark, his awakened soul could see beauties of life and the fullness of God. Sightless, he could see more than many blessed with vision. The Lord crushed him so that He might use him. God's Word brought hope where there was once despair.

God's Word reveals knowledge, wisdom, and truth for this life—the kind of Truth that will set you free.

## Develop a Pattern to Your Life

The beach is my absolute favorite place on the planet. Every year during our family vacation, I love to sit on the balcony of the place we're staying, watch the waves, see the clouds roll in off the ocean, be amazed as schools of dolphins jump and swim by, and wonder at the expanse of stars above us that become visible in the absence of city lights. I sit and marvel at the *awesomeness* of God. It is therapy for my soul, and so refreshing. It is pure bliss to me.

But I couldn't live at the beach. It is fine as a place of extended escape and retreat, but that is not where my home is. Yet that doesn't mean I have to wait a whole year before I can escape, find rest, and be renewed in my amazement at the grandness of our Creator. I need a place I can go in my home too—a regular place of retreat.

In our house, we have a sitting room where I can be found every morning with a cup of coffee and my Bible. There isn't a day that goes by that my boys don't come down the stairs to find me in that spot, spending time with the

Lord and being recharged spiritually after a night of being recharged physically.

Like me, you may have a favorite vacation spot that makes you feel refreshed, but do you have that same spot in your home? You may like to escape to the mountains to get alone with God, but do you have a corner in your living room where you can do that too? It doesn't have to be fancy—it can just be a favorite chair where you spend a few minutes alone before everyone else in your house wakes up. I make it a habit to visit this place every morning because consistency and predictability in the Christian life is crucial to running the race set before us.

Predictability is not always a bad thing. For instance, I tend to use my favorite phrases, talk about my favorite subjects, and bring up my go-to suggestions—to the point that my husband likes to think he can read my mind by saying what I'm about to say before I say it! He thinks he is a great student of people. I think I am just very predictable. The same is probably true for you when it comes to the things that keep showing up in your speech. Our mouths are always on replay in some form or fashion when it comes to the things that work for us or make us feel good. This kind of predictability is good, and it can work out well for us when spiritual disciplines become as expected in our day as our favorite topic.

Of course, while it's helpful that I'm a predictable person, that's not why I practice spiritual disciplines. I practice spiritual disciplines because they were modeled for us by Jesus. He lived purposely. He held to a pattern in His life, frequented similar places, and was accompanied by the same people. Let's look at a pivotal moment in Jesus' ministry that illustrates just how committed He was to following a predictable pattern of living.

The last night of Jesus' life was filled with beauty and memorable moments. He washed His disciples' feet. He foretold His death. He exposed a betrayer in their midst. He told Peter he'd deny Him. But at the climax of this historic night, Jesus did something remarkable, which John 18:1–2 details for us:

> After Jesus had said these things, he went out with his disciples across the Kidron Valley, where there was a garden, and he and his disciples went into it. Judas, who betrayed him, also knew the place, because Jesus *often met there with his disciples.* (emphasis mine)

Get this: Jesus' disciples knew the rhythms of Jesus' life and whereabouts so well that Judas knew exactly where to seek Him out in order to betray Him. Jesus knew it was coming, but found it important to not alter the regularities He'd instilled in His disciples (and also to fulfill His own prophecy about Judas). The verses make it clear: Judas knew where to find Jesus because Jesus had done this very thing many times before. Luke 22:39 tells us that Jesus "went out and made his way *as usual* to the Mount of Olives, and the disciples followed him" (emphasis mine).

Luke points out details like this for us all over the place. Look at the following passages and note the actions Jesus habitually did and the people He routinely surrounded Himself with.

> Luke 21:37: "During the day, he was teaching in the temple, but in the evening he would go out and *spend the night* on what is called the Mount of Olives." (emphasis mine)

> Luke 11:1: "He was *praying in a certain place*, and when he finished, one of his disciples said to him, 'Lord, teach us to pray, just as John also taught his disciples.'" (emphasis mine)

> Luke 9:28: "About eight days after this conversation, he took along Peter, John, and James and *went up on the mountain* to pray" (the Transfiguration account). (emphasis mine)

> Luke 9:18: "While *he was praying in private* and his disciples were with him, he asked them, 'Who do the crowds say that I am?'" (emphasis mine)

> Luke 6:12–13: "During those days he *went out to the mountain to pray* and spent all

night in prayer to God. When daylight came, he summoned his disciples, and he chose twelve of them, whom he also named apostles." (emphasis mine)

Luke 5:16: "Yet *he often withdrew to deserted places* and prayed." (emphasis mine)

Even Mark, in all of his Gospel's conciseness, points out details like this for us:

Mark 1:35–36: "Very *early in the morning, while it was still dark, he got up, went out, and made his way to a deserted place; and there he was praying.* Simon and his companions searched for him, and when they found him they said, 'Everyone is looking for you.'" (emphasis mine)

Over and over again, the disciples knew exactly where to look to find Christ!

The most prominent pattern we see in verses like these is that Jesus "went out"—often very early or while it was still dark, either at the beginning or the end of the day, depending on what the day demanded of Him.

My mom and sister jokingly call me the Time Warden, because I function best on a schedule. I asked my mom one day, "What exactly is it that I do that makes me the time warden?" She said I always give her a time limit when we go shopping or run errands. I didn't even realize I did that until she told me. Then I found myself laughing because it hit me—I totally do that all the time! The way I see it, you either manage your time or your time manages you!

I remember really understanding this principle when my boys were babies. I found myself having to go to bed early if I wanted to safeguard my quiet time in the morning. It took some planning and sacrifice, but I found that if I could be asleep by ten, waking up at six was not impossible. The boys would fuss during the night and unexpected obstacles would keep me from getting rest, but in general, sticking to a plan was helpful. It instilled a pattern in me like muscle memory. If I was going to be serious about spending time with God, I was going to have to make it happen. And with all the demands of being a pastor's wife and a mother, living a patterned life is crucial and, in the end, helpful. Structure helps you manage a demanding life.

Yes, we should pursue a patterned life that has structure and routine to it, especially when it comes to spending time with God, because it's useful and effective and keeps us sane. On top of that, though, there's a better reason we must live out these rhythms, as seen in the gospel accounts: Jesus did the same.

## Plan for Interruptions

In October 2015, when we had just moved to Hendersonville, Tennessee, our worship team had an album release concert. It was one of the first weekends at our new church in our new city, and was the first major event we were a part of as a whole family.

I figured this concert was going to be perfect for my seven- and five-year-old boys, who were tornadoes wrapped in flesh. I was thinking about how perfect this event would be—they'd be able to look at all of the flashing lights, hear all of the loud music, and nobody would look at them if they were moving around to the rhythm of the songs.

All was well and good until the band asked the audience to sit down and took a few minutes to explain where these songs came from and to thank the church for their support. I could sense the storm brewing in my boys. The restlessness began, and only increased. My own aggravation was growing, as was (I'm sure) that of the people around me, and eventually I was simply fed up. I left the first row, stormed out to the lobby with Rig and Ryder in tow, and sat on a chair as they ran their energy out.

We weren't out there for two minutes before a lady walked out with her two children (one of whom is severely handicapped). Her youngest was between my boys' ages, so the three of them immediately started playing together. She and I sat down, and for close to forty minutes we talked and realized we had a lot in common as parents of children with some special needs. She was one of the first friends I made at our church and remains a great friend to this day.

When I look back on that moment, full of frustration at the interruption of what I expected to be a relaxing night, I now think about how grateful I am God had a different plan. He wanted to introduce me to my first friend at my new church by getting us alone in the lobby where we could connect. Sometimes our perfectly thought-out plans can be interrupted—and that's okay. It even happened to Jesus on occasion.

One time Jesus planned to go to a remote place to be alone but was prevented from doing so due to the tremendous crowds. Right before He fed a multitude, in Matthew 14:13–14 the Bible says,

> When Jesus heard about it, he withdrew from there by boat to a remote place to be alone. When the crowds heard this, they followed him on foot from the towns. When he went ashore, he saw a large crowd, had compassion on them, and healed their sick.

He wasn't able to get any alone-time after a long period of intentional ministry, but God used Him and His disciples to feed what may have been 25,000 people! And guess what? After He dismissed the crowd, Matthew tells us that "he went up on the mountain by himself to pray. Well into the night, he was there alone" (v. 23). He couldn't follow through with His plan beforehand, but Jesus tried again. And this time He got what His heart desired, time alone with His Father.

Interruptions aren't always a bad thing. Interruptions could be an opportunity. Kay Warren, in her book *Sacred Privilege,* says, "I wonder if the principle we should grasp is this: sometimes the interrupted is not as important as the interrupter."[3] We should strive to have that daily alone time with God, but we should also be prepared for our plans to be interrupted.

As Robby and I allowed more time to go by, our oldest son began coming to the main church service with me; he now does well sitting next to me! At one point, I wasn't ever sure that would happen. Every week Rig listens to his daddy preach. Of course, he brings Batman, Robin, and any other figure he can fit in his pocket, but I'm okay with that. We're taking baby steps, and I'm not so attached to the end goal of having him sit through a service to let intermediate steps frustrate me.

## Enhancing Your Quality Time with the Father

Years ago, I discovered what my love language is. There is a book on this topic called *The Five Love Languages* by Gary Chapman, which helps you understand how you feel loved and how you demonstrate it to others. The love languages are: Quality Time, Acts of Service, Words of Affirmation, Giving Gifts, and Physical Touch. You can be more than one, but typically one will rise to the top above the rest.

Mine is, by far, Quality Time. I love giving gifts and encouragement, but Quality Time makes me feel loved, adored, and cherished. I feel so important and loved when I get to spend time with Robby, my mom, my kids, or my girlfriends and when they make time to spend with me.

I believe that if we asked Jesus what His love language is, He would most likely say Quality Time. He demonstrated over and over that He wanted to spend quality time with His Father and with His disciples.

Not only did He intentionally withdraw to spend time with God, but He always spent that time in prayer. Prayer is communicating with God—using the time you've set apart to have a conversation with Him. Think about your own prayer life and what it looks like. Many of us speak our prayers, but I also like to write mine. It helps me focus and keeps my mind from wandering. It also helps me create silence and space to allow God to speak to me. It helps me listen and be present in the moment with Him.

Most believers know they should have a quiet time, but many aren't sure exactly what to do and how it should be structured. Before we discuss that, humor me for a moment. Instead of calling this our quiet time, it may help to call it our *quality* time. I will even shorten it to QT. Your QT can consist of a few things: Bible reading/studying, journaling, praying, and memorizing Scripture.

Now hold on. We've spent time already talking about how we use Jesus as an example for what we do, but the last I checked, no one has ever seen Jesus carrying around a Bible or scribbling thoughts and prayers onto a notepad. Let's remember Jesus didn't have His own house to wake up to each day. He couldn't go get in His cozy chair every morning. He often traveled from town to town and stayed in the homes of friends. He didn't have a bookshelf full of resources to help Him study. These are modern inventions, but they help us do something He was adept at without needing them: He meditated on the Word and used that to inform the way He spoke to the Father.

As a devout Jew, Jesus would have committed enormous passages of Scripture (what we call the Old Testament) to memory. It was part of the formal education every Jewish male child would have received. He frequently referred to these passages with verbal cues, like quoting the first line of a psalm or outright referencing a story His audience would have been familiar with. Because He had hidden God's Word in His heart, He carried it with Him every-where—especially to those places to which He intentionally retreated in order to spend quality time with the Father. Not to mention He was the walking Word, as John tells us in John 1:14, "The Word became flesh and dwelt among us."

Most of us don't have all of Scripture committed to memory, but we have the same basic requirements Jesus did. We need a remote place. A detached space where we can decompress and dive into His Word.

For me it is a chair in my little sitting area. I have a chair and ottoman and I have my bookshelf with lots of my books, numerous Bibles, and a lamp. That's my spot. It's where I meet with God every morning. It is the best part of my day and what I look forward to when I go to bed each night. I get so excited to go to sleep so I can wake up early and go meet with the Lord. It is my cozy, dimly lit, special place. My dogs crawl up next to me while I read and often my children come down when they wake up and greet me with morning kisses as they crawl in my lap and talk about whether they slept well or not.

Maybe the chair-thing isn't quite right for you. Maybe you need to sit outside. Or perhaps you need to go on a walk everyday because getting your blood moving makes your soul move too. Or maybe you're a person who needs to pray out loud to keep your thoughts together. Whatever it may look like for you, I implore you to do as Jesus did and as I have learned to do: find that place where you can be regularly refreshed.

## Invest in Others

The final thing we will note from Jesus' spiritual habits is that when He was not retreating to be alone with the Father, He lived His life among the same people.

Jesus ministered in three groups. First, He taught in crowds. He would teach masses from a boat and feed thousands on hillsides. He would be among the citizens healing and performing miracles.

While He would engage with large crowds on occasion, the second group—his disciples—is where He spent most of His time. Most of His ministry was spent around the twelve disciples He'd sought out and determined to invest in. This was His community. He lived, traveled, and ministered with these men and He modeled for them what living on purpose looks like. In many of the passages we read earlier, it's clear that He had been with the disciples, and in some cases the disciples were present with Him in the remote places. The verses we read at the start of this chapter show us that He went to the garden often with these men.

After the Twelve, we see that He had an even more intimate relationship with a third group—who many know as "the three." In His inner circle were Peter, James, and John. This core group was where He modeled a lifestyle of discipleship. These three were included in numerous accounts that the other disciples weren't. When we read about Jesus on the Mount of Transfiguration, the healing of Peter's mother-in-law, the healing of Jairus's daughter, and the garden of Gethsemane before His arrest, we see that He was with His closest inner circle.

Christians have gotten fairly good at sharing the gospel over the years, but we aren't good at sharing our lives. The disciples—especially the three closest to him—didn't have that problem with Jesus. They knew the pattern of His life, they knew where He went to be alone and spend time with His Father. This, like the practice of getting alone with the Father, is something we can emulate today.

We have already noted that you need a regular daily time with the Lord, but it is equally important to allow others into your life so that you can share it with them. You may have a past that you feel shame from. You may feel like you are not special like others you've met. I can absolutely relate to you in both of those cases, but here is the deal: If you are a born-again believer, you have already been saved by God's grace and redeemed by His blood and forgiven from your former ways. You have already received the gift of the Holy Spirit to strengthen you in the areas you feel deficient. More than ever, we need authentic, transparent believers who share their stories and give glory to God because of it.

As we journey through this book together, we're going to explore this very thing: how to invest your life into other women in the same way Jesus did. By using the Word you know, the work He has done, and the empowerment of the Holy Spirit, you can be a disciple that makes disciples. Whether you are a leader or a participant, a D-Group will benefit everyone. The group will keep you accountable. They will encourage you to grow closer to the Father. They will strengthen your spiritual disciplines. And you will do the same for them.

It is a process called discipleship, and it is a process that will radically change your life. This book is going to lay out in plain words exactly how you can be involved in it, just as Jesus was with His own disciples.

# 2

# Discipleship Is a Lifestyle

One of the most frustrating and intimidating parts of going to a foreign country is figuring out how to communicate. It is hard to feel more alone than being in a crowd of people of whom you have no idea how to even ask simple questions: What's good to eat? Where is the bathroom? Is this road safe to take?

What is even more frustrating is being somewhere for a specific purpose but not being able to express yourself. If you are in front of a large crowd of people who are waiting to hear a message from you but you have no idea how to speak their language, you will feel like a fish out of water, gasping for breath. You will feel small, isolated, helpless. It helps to have a translator—someone who can hear what you're saying and put it in words that your audience understands—but it is so much more effective to have a common ground with the people to whom you are trying to communicate. You have to be speaking the same language.

For many reasons, discipleship has been misconstrued over the years. Some have tried to reduce it to a program: something you only do once a week with a small group of ladies. That's part of it, but it's not the whole picture. Before we can develop that picture, though, we need to get on the same footing. We need to make sure we're speaking the same language.

My husband and I founded our ministry, Replicate Ministries, many years ago. Replicate Ministries is a disciple-making ministry in which we provide teaching, training, and resources to help equip churches with a disciple-making strategy for their context. We have met every single week for years to discuss discipleship in our specific church and in churches at large.

Through much prayer and discussion with our team over the years, we adopted this definition of discipleship: *Discipleship is intentionally equipping believers with the Word of God through accountable relationships empowered by the Holy Spirit in order to replicate faithful followers of Christ.*

Another term that will be helpful to define is a D-Group. A D-Group is what we call discipleship groups. They consist of three to five same-gender individuals (men meet with men, women with women) that meet for twelve to eighteen months. These groups read the Bible, journal, pray, and memorize Scripture, among other things, with the intention and expectation of each person doing the same thing later on with others.

As you make disciples through a D-Group, there are three major sources to draw from: the Word of God, the work of God in one's life, and the wonder of God, which is the Holy Spirit that lives inside of us as believers.

A seminary professor once told me that you can't draw from an empty well. That has stuck in my mind for many years. If the well is empty and dry there is nothing to pour out. Let's begin by filling those wells with the Word.

## God's Word

Look at some of the ways the power of God's Word is described:

> For just as rain and snow fall from heaven and do not return there without saturating the earth and making it germinate and sprout, and providing seed to sow and food to eat, so my word that comes from my mouth will not return to me empty, but it will accomplish what I please and will prosper in what I send it to do. (Isa. 55:10–11)

Also:

> For the word of God is living and effective and sharper than any double-edged sword, penetrating as far as the separation of soul and spirit, joints and marrow. It is able to

judge the thoughts and intentions of the
heart. (Heb. 4:12)

These are verses I repeat constantly to women I disciple. The Word of God is living, active, refreshing; it is not
dead, stationary, lifeless, immobile, or passive. It's alive
and breathing and working to accomplish the purpose
Almighty God has already set forth!

The Word of God is where we learn about who God
is and what He has done from the beginning of time. It is
where we learn the gospel: the good news of Jesus Christ
coming down from heaven to die for our sins, and about how
God raised Him to life three days later. We gain knowledge,
insight, wisdom, and truth from the Bible, and it serves as
the foundation for our entire faith. It determines the course
of our life, and all decisions we make should be centered on
what God's Word says. Julie Manning said in her book *My
Heart*, "We can only view this life through the lens of the
gospel of Jesus to the extent in which we know and believe
the gospel itself."[4] We can only have a biblical worldview to
the extent we know the Bible.

My ultimate goal and desire in any discipleship relationship is for the ladies to walk away with a love for God's
Word. If they walk away with that, they will not be able to
help but make disciples! It will flow so naturally from their
heart and mind. There is a quote attributed to Antoine de
Saint-Exupéry that says, "If you want to build a ship, don't
drum up people to collect wood and don't assign them tasks
and work but rather teach them to long for the endless
immensity of the sea."[5] As you make disciples, you want to

create an atmosphere for a deep love and passion for God's Word. If you succeed in helping women long for God's Word, they will always make disciples.

Scripture is how we learn who God is. We learn about His character, His love and mercy, His constant pursuit of us, His wrath, His forgiveness, and so much more. As I approach Scripture each morning, I begin by praying Psalm 119:18–19, "Open my eyes so that I may contemplate wondrous things from your instruction. I am a resident alien on earth; do not hide your commands from me." I want God to reveal and speak to me, but I am also filled with a craving to learn more about Him and see how I can apply His Word to my life today. I want to know more about His character, His sovereignty, His history, His people, and His redemptive plan that is traced through every page.

No time in God's Word is ever wasted because you are learning more about Him and His story. God's Word is where you learn how to navigate life through the lens of absolute truth. Life changes, sometimes daily, and a dependence on God's words to us is necessary. My husband always says, "The Word works if you work the Word."

## God's Work

See, discipleship is not just a thing you do once a week, it is a lifestyle. I hope and pray you get that if nothing else. It's an all day, every day life and mentality. It flows naturally from the heart of a woman who loves God and can't help sharing about what her Savior has done for her. She will want to tell those stories to other women and encourage them to have similar experiences. I love to process how God has worked in my own life. Even more so, I love helping women value the very intentional works of God in their own lives.

We all have countless testimonies in our lives of things the Lord has done. Some of these are great, joyful, mountaintop experiences. Some of these are also painful ones that have stretched and pulled us in ways we never expected or even wanted. However, nothing that God allows ever goes to waste. He has done a work in each of our hearts and lives that is unique to each of us and it's worth sharing and retelling. The gospel came to you because it is heading to someone else—your life experiences happened to you so that you can apply what you've learned through them to others. Your life experiences came to you but weren't meant to stay with you. They are intended to be shared.

Again, Kay Warren states in her book *Sacred Privilege*:

> There is always going to be a temptation to go back into the box and not tell your story, but you have a story that's worth telling. You actually encourage other people when you use your own story. Has it ever occurred to you that you are not living your life just for yourself? That the things that happen to you—the things you've gone through and struggled with—are actually meant to encourage others?[6]

She hit the nail on the head!

The past often helps us in the present. If we learn from our history, it can help us today. In 1 Corinthians 10:11 Paul writes, "These things happened to them as examples, and they were written for our instruction, on whom the ends of the ages have come." Paul is talking to the church in Corinth and reminding them of Israel's past. He explains that these things happened as an example and were written down to help them in the present. They were to learn from the past by looking at what happened to those who had come before them. That is how our life works today. Things in our past should not only help us in the present, but we should be willing to share those things to help others. Our experiences are examples of lessons learned if we let them be.

I will never forget when we started noticing our oldest son having some struggles in school. We noticed a few things even before he was in preschool, but since he was our first child, we didn't have anything to compare it to. We weren't exactly sure what was normal and what wasn't. He was young, only three at the time, and the doctor wanted to wait to evaluate him. Being he was a boy and it could be his age and general immaturity, his pediatrician wanted to wait until he was at least four. By the time he was four there was no denying that we needed an evaluation. We had a conference with a teacher a few months after school started who said, "Rig is so smart but there are times I ask him to do something and he says no." It wasn't an issue of defiance, but of the fact that he couldn't process what she was telling him. When she said the word "process" my heart started beating so fast. I remember thinking, "This is a big deal."

We noted numerous behaviors, but when we met with the doctor after his fourth birthday, this is how I described him: "Rig is academically above everyone in the class, but he is socially below them all. He is socially unaware." After all the evaluations and tests, and when all was said and done, Rig was diagnosed with Sensory Processing Disorder and most likely ADHD.

Like any mom at this point, I was going through some extreme emotions and struggles. I cried a lot as I tried to process what this meant for him and what we could do to help. I asked all the questions in my mind and heart. Would he have this forever? Would medication help, and should we try it? How on earth will we navigate this?

At the church where my husband pastored at the time, we had a Christian school that Rig attended. We had to pull him from the school and enrolled him in a school that would help with his social skills, which broke my heart. Rig's current school was familiar and comfortable. It was known for excellence. It had the same namesake as the church my husband pastored—and he had an office upstairs, so he was close in case the worst happened. It was safe. Secure.

But at the same time, we had begun therapy with a woman who would change our lives. It was at her prompting that we switched schools, so I trusted her judgment even if it was hard. Within the span of that first very emotional week, God confirmed we had made the right move in changing schools. I will never forget picking him up on the first day and being greeted by his teacher with this statement: "Let me tell you what Rig did today. He read a book from memory to the class!"

Let me tell you, I burst into tears. I had gone from hearing every week what Rig *couldn't* do to hearing what Rig *could* do. There is nothing like having someone else see the beauty in your child that you see.

In the midst of those first few weeks as I was feeling quite alone in our new experience of having a child with special needs, I received an email from a mom. Her daughter was in the same K-4 class that we had just pulled Rig from. She was also a church member and I knew her only a little at the time. God had prompted her to reach out to me even though she had no clue what I was going through. She told me in this letter all about the struggles her daughter was having in school, and that she just didn't know what to do. She explained how hard it was being in this situation. She wasn't sure what to do about evaluations, therapies, medication, and school.

As I sat there reading her letter, I was crying my eyes out (a theme of those first few weeks). I couldn't believe within the first few weeks of going through this, God was sending someone in my life experiencing the same exact thing. I was reading my life in her words! I immediately called Robby and (through tears) read him the letter. I hated that she was experiencing this, but at the same time I was thankful because I knew I wasn't alone, and neither was she. God had provided someone with whom I could talk and share these experiences.

Of course, I immediately contacted her back and we got together to share about our situations. A year after this, this same mom would be in one of my discipleship groups! In a way that only God can, He connected us.

I realized pretty quickly that God was giving me a platform with moms who had these precious kids with special needs. This work of God in our life brought moms out of the woodwork who were experiencing some of the same challenges we were. Many were afraid to even take the first step.

Listen closely: if we allow our fear to paralyze us, nothing gets handled and the situation will become worse. I want to be a woman who operates on faith, not fear. I chose to trust God above anyone and anything else. I knew early on that I was going to be Rig's greatest advocate and support. I wanted to be his biggest encourager and confidence builder. As I put him to bed every single night I said this to him, "Rig, do you know that God created you just how He wants you and He has a very special plan for your life?" Not only did I want to encourage my son, I also wanted to share what God was doing and teaching me with other moms in this same situation. There was joy and hope in being able to say, "I understand a little of what you are going through. I know God has a purpose and a plan for you and your precious child."

There were still days of struggles and emotions, of course. But even still, God would remind me of what He was doing. Finally, one day the light bulb went off. God's will for Rig is GOD'S will, and GOD'S will can't be wrong. I began to meditate on that, knowing that nothing happens by accident. God knew exactly what He was doing. This wasn't any mistake or mishap. This didn't happen by accident or catch God off guard.

Psalm 139:15–16 says, "My bones were not hidden from you when I was made in secret, when I was formed in the depths of the earth. Your eyes saw me when I was formless; all my days were written in your book and planned before a single one of them began." Can you believe that on *that* day of struggle *this* passage happened to be my quiet-time reading? Of course, nothing just happens. I had been following a reading plan for the year. Only God in His divine wisdom had preordained this passage to fall on this day. God was very intentional in His design and plan for Rig. And I praise Him for it!

That is the thing about God's work in one's life: it is God's work, not ours. His will can't be wrong for you or anyone you know. Sometimes His will isn't pleasant and it takes us places we don't want to be, but it is never wrong.

Have you ever heard of the poem "Welcome to Holland"? A friend shared it with me back when we were in uncharted territory of Rig's diagnosis. It was an encouragement to me and I hope it is for you as well. A mom was asked to write what it is like to have a child with a disability, and this was what she penned:

> I am often asked to describe the experience
> of raising a child with a disability—to try to
> help people who have not shared that unique

experience to understand it, to imagine how it would feel. It's like this . . .

When you're going to have a baby, it's like planning a fabulous vacation trip—to Italy. You buy a bunch of guidebooks and make your wonderful plans. The Coliseum, the Michelangelo David, the gondolas in Venice. You may learn some handy phrases in Italian. It's all very exciting.

After months of eager anticipation, the day finally arrives. You pack your bags and off you go. Several hours later, the plane lands. The stewardess comes in and says, "Welcome to Holland."

"Holland?!" you say. "What do you mean, Holland?" I signed up for Italy! I'm supposed to be in Italy. All my life I've dreamed of going to Italy.

But there's been a change in the flight plan. They've landed in Holland and there you must stay.

The important thing is that they haven't taken you to some horrible, disgusting, filthy place, full of pestilence, famine, and disease. It's just a different place.

So you must go out and buy a new guidebook. And you must learn a whole new language. And you will meet a whole new group of people you would never have met.

It's just a different place. It's slower paced than Italy, less flashy than Italy. But after you've been there for a while and you catch your breath, you look around, and you begin to notice that Holland has windmills, Holland has tulips, Holland even has Rembrandts.

But everyone you know is busy coming and going from Italy, and they're all bragging about what a wonderful time they had there. And for the rest of your life you will say, "Yes, that's where I was supposed to go. That's what I had planned."

The pain of that will never, ever, go away, because the loss of that dream is a very significant loss.

But if you spend your life mourning the fact that you didn't get to Italy, you may never be free to enjoy the very special, the very lovely things about Holland.[7]

by Emily Perl Kingsley

This is a beautiful thought: we grieve the loss of what we thought life was going to be and give that to God. We grieve one dream, but we gain another. Psalm 119:68 says, "You are good, and You do what is good; teach me your statutes."

I was talking to a dear friend one day about this and about discipleship, and she taught me a principle about discipling women that has stuck with me. "You are teaching women to be a good steward of their life experiences." Frankly, I couldn't have said it better. I never thought of it as being a good steward of what God has done in our lives, but the same is always true: What has happened to you, be it your acceptance of the gospel or an experience you didn't think you could get through, is as much for the next person as it is for you. We are to take these things and pass them on, not hoard them for ourselves.

This is what we need to grasp and understand. Our life is a lesson. The very things we want to avoid, pain and suffering, are the very things God uses to shape us. Just as we have physical scars from pain we have suffered in our lives due to accidents and injuries, we also have spiritual scars. Spiritual scars are those things in life that have forever marked us. They have forever changed us. We are different because of them. Some of these we had no control over. And then some of these may be a result of something we did or didn't do. Sometimes we have to learn the hard way instead of learning the Lord's way.

I love music. I love many genres of music, actually. Oldies, Christian, Jazz, '80s Rock, and Country to name just a few. I grew up listening to oldies and country. And I live outside of Nashville, so of course I listen to country now. There is a song by Miranda Lambert called "Tin Man." She is singing from a broken heart and telling the tin man he doesn't really need the heart he is in search of. At the end of the song she tells the tin man if he doesn't mind the scars, he can give her his armor and she will give him her heart. When our heart breaks we may wish we didn't have a heart either. It's the whole beauty-from-ashes concept. Our suffering, our spiritual scars, shape us tremendously.

A couple of years ago, in one of my D-Groups, we had an intense year of life experiences we walked through together. One of us lost a parent, one's husband was diagnosed with cancer, one's husband had abandoned her and her daughter, one had lost a child the year before, two of us had children with disabilities, and one was watching her best friends in all the world deal with a cancer diagnosis. In this same group we also had a friend who was a brand-new believer when she started with us! It was incredible to walk alongside these ladies for a year and a half. You can't imagine the closeness we had as we lived life together and depended on one another through these trials. Life isn't easy. Praise God we don't have to go through it alone if we choose to share our lives with others!

Here are a few helpful ways to begin sharing your life with others.

First, you need to *remember* what God has done. Why? Because God Himself is a God of remembrance, and we want to be like Him, don't we? All throughout Scripture, He remembers His people and calls for the people to remember Him. Here's what's interesting: when God remembers, there is always an action associated with it. Lois Tverberg helps to explain this concept in her article entitled "How Can God Forget Sins?"[8]

Tverberg explains that in the English language, to remember is to simply recall a memory or bring an idea to mind. However in the Hebrew language, the word *zakhar* means not only to remember, but it also includes the *actions* that go along with remembering.[9] Scripture is filled with examples of this:

> Genesis 8:1: "God *remembered* Noah . . . God *caused a wind to pass* over the earth, and the water began to subside." (emphasis mine)

> Genesis 19:29: "So it was, when God destroyed the cities of the plain, he *remembered* Abraham and *brought Lot out* of the middle of the upheaval when he demolished the cities where Lot had lived." (emphasis mine)

> Genesis 30:22: "Then God *remembered* Rachel. He listened to her and *opened her womb*." (emphasis mine)

> The Israelites were told in Exodus 20:8 to "*Remember* the Sabbath day, to *keep it* holy." Their remembering was an action of rest and reflection.

> In Joshua 4, God told His people to build stone memorials so that when they passed by them they would *remember* what God had done so they could *tell* the coming generations.

Your journey is worth remembering because it reveals how God has worked in your life. You remembering God reveals how God remembered you (and *acted* on your behalf)!

Actively remembering—recalling something to your mind—is important, but it is even more poignant in relation to its opposite: forgetting. As we remember what God has done, let's also remember one of the most fantastic things God does—more specifically, what He *doesn't* do. He doesn't remember our sins. So what does that mean? That He does not *act* on them either.

If remembering is an intentional action, that gives us an interesting picture of what God says in Isaiah 43:25: "I sweep away your transgressions for my own sake and *remember* your sins no more" (emphasis mine). This doesn't mean that God *can't* remember, it means that God chooses not to act on it once we have been forgiven by the blood of His Son.

This completely blows my mind over and over again. Although I deserve punishment, I won't receive it because in Christ, God has intentionally decided to not remember (and therefore not do anything wrathful) the sins He has forgiven me from. Remembering what God has done and what He has forgotten increases our loyalty to and love for Him.

Sometimes actively remembering things we've gone through (or even things we've been forgiven from) can be a painful experience. There are things in my life that still have painful emotions attached to them. However, when I reflect on these, pray, and depend on God, it helps bring healing in those areas. At times we need to experience that healing over and over again.

We tend to be forgetful people, don't we? We can forget God's provision, His forgiveness, His strength, His grace, His direction, His goodness, His healing, and His miraculous ways of working out things in a way that only He can. I know that in my own life, if I am experiencing a struggle or even shame from my past, I must remind myself that God has forgiven me. I must remind myself that He is my only source of hope. I must remind myself that He is always there and never leaves me or forsakes me. I must remember Him.

What do you need to remember about God today? Think back on what God has already done in your life and remind yourself of His goodness and grace.

Second, once you have remembered, you should *share* what He has done. Just like God's people in the book of Joshua, retelling is our action paired with remembering. When you feel prompted by the Lord, obey Him and share what He has done in your life. This not only helps you obey God's Word when it comes to remembrance, it helps you become more like God over time. You start remembering the way *God* remembers things.

When we pulled Rig from school in order to put him somewhere that was more equipped to help him, our desire was that God would allow us to come back to our school for K–5. Because Rig has a September birthday, we knew he would do K–4 twice, giving us some extra time to help him develop. So he ended up being at the other school for one and a half years. When it came time for K–5, we had him retested to see if he could go back to our church's school.

You can't know the excitement when the testing came back positive—he could return! It was a clear answer to prayer. All in all, we did therapy for three and a half years. I sat in every session with him to learn how to handle certain things, understand how to communicate with him, and celebrate little breakthroughs. He isn't symptom-free today, but God has done a mighty work in his little life and ours as well. I am so thankful for what God has taught me through my Riggy!

He is about to turn nine as I write this, and I can't imagine him being any different than this perfect way God has created him. As we saw in the previous section, God's *Word* is where we gain knowledge, wisdom, and truth. Now we see that God's *work* in our lives is where we learn to apply those things. As I read Psalm 139:13–16 one morning, I found myself inserting Rig's name. Through tears God was reminding me of who He is and what He is doing.

> For it was you who created Rig's inward parts; you knit Rig together in my womb. I will praise you because Rig has been remarkably and wondrously made. Your works are wondrous, and I know this very well. Rig's bones were not hidden from you when he was made in secret, when he was formed in the depths of the earth. Your eyes saw Rig when he was formless; all his

days were written in your book and planned
before a single one of them began.

## God's Wonder

Part of the majesty of God is that He is full of mystery. He is vast and timeless, infinitely creative and infinitely merciful in ways that we can never truly wrap our minds around. That's okay—we can sometimes use things that we do understand in order to help get a picture of what He's like. Seeing God's aspects played out in miniature before our eyes helps us see them at large in the universe around us. It is good for us to dwell in that constant wonder of God. And one of the most wondrous, but most misunderstood aspects of God is the third person of the Trinity—the Holy Spirit.

Sometimes Christians don't spend a lot of time talking about the Holy Spirit, but I believe that's a mistake. I won't begin to say I know all there is to know about the Holy Spirit, but Scripture has guided me in a few things I can be sure of.

Before starting, we must begin by noting that the Holy Spirit is a *person*, not a force or a realm or a thing. Scripture (and Jesus Himself) refers to the Spirit as a *He*, not an *it*. Though His role in our lives looks different than the Father's or Jesus Christ's, He is just as much a personal being as they are. The Holy Spirit shares the same essence as God, because He *is* God, and God is personal.

Now that we have that part covered, we note that the Holy Spirit offers us His personal *presence*. The very presence of God, in fact. When Jesus told His disciples that He'd be departing, He said, "It is for your benefit that I go away, because if I don't go away the Counselor will not come to you. If I go, I will send him to you" (John 16:7). Jesus actually said that having this Counselor—this Spirit—with us was *better* than having the physical Jesus on earth! Is that the sort of presence you feel when you've heard about the Spirit in the past?

Scripture goes on to tell us that this Spirit is offered as a *gift* to us, a sort of promise and guarantee that we will inherit eternal life and spend forever and ever with Jesus (Eph. 1:13–14). It also shows that upon conversion to Christ, the Holy Spirit was received by Jews (like the disciples) and Gentiles (like in Acts 10:45) alike, as proof that salvation is for all who believe in Jesus. Please do not underestimate the significance of the Spirit; it's the very presence of the Lord dwelling inside of you!

But the Spirit is more than just a feeling or a comfort; He does not just bring God's presence in your life, but His *power*. When Jesus ascended after having been with the disciples, He promised that they would receive power when the Holy Spirit comes (Acts 1:8).

This power has been a source of some debate in many circles throughout history, but one thing we can all agree on is that no matter what the power of the Spirit is doing in any given moment, it is always used to declare the greatness of God in some form or fashion. The Holy Spirit is not a Spirit of confusion or of turmoil, but of clarity and strength: clarity of who God is, and strength to proclaim it. In Acts 2, that power caused people to speak in the languages of the many people represented in the streets of Jerusalem, so that they could all hear the Good News in their own tongue. He is the same Spirit that empowered Stephen to preach, and Paul to preach after that. He is the same Spirit that gives you the words about God even if you have no idea what to say. In a million different ways and at a million different moments, He helps you declare God's greatness.

It comforts me to think about who the Spirit is and what He does in my life. I'm the type of person who hates goodbyes. I always have been. I can remember when Robby would travel back and forth to school (which he used to have to do every week when we were newly married and in ministry), and I couldn't stand it. I hated saying goodbye, even when I knew he'd be back. When my parents would come visit us and they would be backing out of the driveway to head home after a week's stay, there I was starting to cry as their car drove away.

I can't imagine standing there on the mountainside that day in Acts 1 when Jesus was about to ascend into heaven. I read this chapter and my heart strings are tugged as if I'm there with the eleven disciples, wanting to hang on to every day and every last minute they have together. Jesus is departing from them again. But His was not a bitter goodbye, for someone amazing came in His place. The Spirit is our counselor, companion, guide, teacher, and source of wisdom as we invest our lives into others. And the Bible reminds us of this in Matthew 28:20: "'Remember, I am with you always, to the end of the age.'"

Every believer has the Holy Spirit as her counselor, which John tells us in John 14:26. We are enabled to do what God has called us to do by the gift of the Holy Spirit within us. You and I need His wisdom and discernment throughout the entire process of making disciples. In order to fill that need, Jesus has fully equipped us to be coworkers in reaching the ends of the earth by sending us His Spirit. He is much like the air we breathe. We can't see the air we breathe; it's invisible, yet we need it to survive.

He is our constant companion that goes everywhere we do. We may not be able to see Him, but He is always there with us, indwelling us and providing the power we need to advance God's Kingdom. And unlike other companions we may have in this life, the Holy Spirit will never leave us. We are sealed and indwelt by Him. There aren't restrictions as to when and where He can accompany us. That is good news to us today! He is our constant Counselor as we wait to be with Jesus for eternity.

We must remember that, yes, we will go home one day. We will go home and be united with Jesus. Our faith will be fulfilled and become sight and we will live in the presence of Jesus forever! In the meantime though, aren't you glad you never have to be alone? We have God's Word speaking to us, the record of what God has done in our lives to remind us, and the Holy Spirit's presence always with us. On top of that, we have one another. In a discipleship relationship, we exist to remind one another of these truths daily.

In order to make disciples who make disciples who make disciples, you have to first be a disciple yourself. In order to lead others well, you have to lead yourself well. As you make disciples you are drawing from three major sources: God's Word (learn it and live it), God's work (remember it, reflect, remind, and retell), and God's wonder—the Holy Spirit (living in total surrender and daily dependence).

# 3

# Pray and Plan

This may sound too good to be true, but discipleship is one of those things that is going to change your life forever. Living wholly surrendered to carrying out Jesus' final words ushers you into a life filled with the kind of joy nothing from this world can provide.

The purpose of this book is to help you get started as soon as today.

We've already begun to see the benefits of what discipleship can bring. Getting into a rhythm and pattern that revolves around the Word of God is the only first step you *need* in order to start making disciples. You do not need to be a master disciple-maker; the only requirement is that you be one step ahead of the people you are discipling.

I hope in the following chapters to equip you with an effective strategy for making disciples who will in turn replicate and make more disciples. Let's begin with the most important part: prayer.

## Pray for Potential Women

I cannot stress this hard enough: before you can begin making disciples, you need to pray for the ladies that God will lead you to disciple. Pray for two things: for God to lead you to women, and for God to send women to you. If we are looking to Christ as our example, we see that He invited all of His disciples to journey with Him. None of the Twelve came to Jesus and said, "I want to live life with You." Jesus approached and asked them all. But before He approached them, He prayed for them. All night actually.

Luke 6:12 tells us that Jesus "spent all night in prayer" directly before selecting twelve from among the disciples. We have reason to believe Jesus had somewhat of a following at this point beyond the twelve we know as His disciples. He had a bit of notoriety among the locals—at the very least as a rabbi and teacher. He'd probably encountered most of those he called at one point or another, because they knew enough about Him to drop what they were doing and come when He called them. You have the same opportunity; you have a pool of people around you in various areas of your life who may only know you by name or reputation. Pray as Jesus did before inviting some of them into a discipleship relationship with you.

As you are praying, be thinking about the areas of influence you already have in your life. You may have connections in a Life Group or Sunday school class, friendships with neighbors, old friends from college, newly/nearly married ladies in your circles, young or single moms, co-workers, young professionals or college women, classroom moms of your children, high school girls, and so on. Ask yourself whether you already feel and sense a leading toward a certain group of ladies. Follow where you already have a passion to serve.

Some of you may be a minister's wife. To you I would suggest getting together with other staff wives at your husband's church. I have always invited staff wives to be a part of my D-Groups in the past, but a few years ago I did a group with all staff wives, and it was incredibly beneficial. It was especially helpful for me because we had just transitioned to a new church so our leadership team wives did not all know each other. We journeyed together for a year and loved every minute. Living life in the ministry can be difficult, and this relationship will be deeply encouraging for all of you.

You don't have to have a group of women all in the same season or stage of life. If you want to mix it up and have a variety of ages and stages, that is fine too. I have a friend in her early thirties who has discipled a few twenty-year-olds, a few ladies in their forties, and a few ladies in their sixties and seventies. There isn't a right or wrong way to do this. Common interests, experiences, or ages bring us together and make us feel connected, but they are certainly not required.

I always encourage those in my groups as they begin to think of ladies to disciple to add potential names on a list and pray through them. Most of my groups meet from January to December, but around summertime is when I encourage them to begin thinking and praying through some people to invite. This gives us several months' worth of discipleship under our belts and leaves us with several months to go as we begin preparing to launch out—and we soak it all in prayer.

If I'm being honest, my antennas are always up for discipleship. When I meet ladies and have conversations, I am often thinking to myself, "I would really like to get to know this person. I wonder if she would be interested in meeting for a D-Group?" I will add her name to a list of women I have been thinking and praying over, and then watch how God either confirms or eliminates those names for some reason. Sometimes they move. Sometimes they get invited into a different D-Group. Sometimes they even approach me. God has a way of bringing D-Groups together as He sees fit. This is all the more reason to bathe the process in prayer.

One last note about the type of people to look for. As you pray through ladies to invite, look for women of F.A.I.T.H.: Faithful, Available, Intentional, Teachable, and Hungry. Are they faithful in the little things? Are they open to being used by God? Do they regularly meet with other believers in church or in a Life Group? Do they have a teachable spirit or are they know-it-alls? Do they have a desire to grow closer to the Lord and practice accountability?

Ideally you are looking for three to five (maybe six) women to journey with you. This is the perfect group size for a D-Group. It is not too small and not too big. Also, you want to avoid meeting with these women one-on-one only— it is not as effective as meeting in a group. You can meet one-on-one outside of group time, but not *instead* of group time. I do one-on-ones all the time, whether that means going to lunch, grabbing coffee, or working out together. However, I don't do one-on-ones *only*. We all commit to meeting as a group every week, and occassionally doing one-on-ones with each other too.

Often when you are meeting one-on-one only, the replication rate is extremely low. This is because many times the disciple looks at the disciple-maker as the quintessential standard of a Christian—a person that they can't measure up to—because they aren't introduced to the diversity of personalities and giftings that come along with God's local body of believers. Meeting in a small group where everyone is contributing and participating helps to dissolve that issue.

Potential women are all around you. Find them and pray for them—you never know what kind of plan God has for you in their lives.

## Plan Your Process

I live by the saying, "If you fail to plan, you plan to fail." If I want to accomplish anything on a daily basis, I have to have a plan. When I go to the grocery store, I have a list (usually written in the order I'll encounter the items). If I am running errands, I have a list of the places I need to go (usually numbered in order from farthest away to closest to home). When I have a pile of work to do, I check items off the list as I get it done. And I love to check items off my list!

Some people are better than others at winging it and accomplishing everything that needs to get done perfectly, but that is certainly not me. And winging it only works for so long before you forget something or have to leave something off because you couldn't get to it in time.

One of my best friends, Kim, and I go to a particular outlet mall once or twice a year because it has some of our favorite stores that you can't find just anywhere. We live two and a half hours away from each other, so we plan a trip when we are able to carve out an entire day. These outlets are two hours from where Kim lives so we know we are in for a long day of driving and shopping. We get at least four hours of driving and talking time and we can normally shop for about three hours once we get there. We look forward to these trips because we get to spend the whole day together!

Since we have a limited time at the shops, we decide beforehand what our plan is. We have it down to a science at this point. However, if we just showed up and decided to wing it we would never get to the places we enjoy going to the most and time would be wasted wandering around. The same principle applies to discipling women. We need a plan if we don't want to get sidetracked by something less important than the task at hand.

A few things you want to consider in detail for a D-Group are: a time frame, information to cover, and essential-versus-optional resources to include.

## Time Frame

A typical time frame to meet with a group is twelve to eighteen months, but this time frame can be flexible. If you are meeting with college students, your time frame may be different since college terms go by semester. In this case you may choose to meet with the same group for two semesters, taking the summer off. Another one of my closest friends, Lori, disciples college girls every year. She journeys with them sometimes for three or even four semesters. She has such a heart for these young women at such a pivotal point and time in their lives. Can you imagine someone walking along side of you when you were in college during those crucial years, pointing you toward God? What a gift that would be to the college women in your life!

I have done D-Groups both for twelve and eighteen months, and they each have their trade-offs. During the course of the eighteen-month group, we were able to read the entire Bible in extremely manageable chunks. What made it tricky was maintaining steam for the last six months. You can feel like you are dragging everyone along a bit. I would recommend eighteen months only for those who are up for the task of meeting for an extended period of time and reading the Bible in its entirety.

For most, however, we've found over the last decade of disciple-making that twelve months is the sweet spot. By the end of that time the ladies are getting excited to replicate and are ready to make disciples themselves. Of course, I say "ready," but many will not be jumping at the chance of doing their own group because they have loved spending

the last twelve months together. By the end of a year walking alongside others, it's hard to part ways and begin again
with a new group. I try encouraging the ladies I disciple to
channel that desire to stay together into a desire to replicate the same kind of connection in other women.

Keep in mind, too, that just because you replicate
doesn't mean your previous relationships end. You will be
forming lifelong friendships with women engaged in the
same mission you are.

Not only do the relationships live on longer, the necessity for ongoing discipleship for the leader is just as necessary as for the participants. Again, discipleship is a lifestyle.
It doesn't start and stop. It isn't on and then off. It's a way of
life. I have discipleship groups every single year because
I need it. For my own spiritual health and growth it is a
necessity. I honestly cannot imagine my life any other way.

The group functions as a unit. Even though I am the
leader and investing in the ladies in my group, they are also
investing in me. They teach and share through what they
are hearing and learning from God. I let our journals drive
our conversation each week. I am being invested in as I
am investing in others. You don't need to have two groups
for the purpose of you being the leader in one, and then
another where someone is leading you. Instead, pour into
one another. And for the purpose of getting to know those
older than you in the faith, it's always wise to have access
to more seasoned women in the faith whom you can call and
seek counsel when needed. I have a few women like that in

my life. I am not in groups with them, but it is an informal kind of discipleship.

And let's remember: as we commit our time to formal D-Groups that we are leading as well as consistent access to older saints in the faith, we are simultaneously *not* committing that time to relationships that aren't healthy for us. I have to say this. Now more than ever, men and women in ministry are falling due to sin. It causes me to wonder if they were living in community? Were they regularly in the Word of God? I know discipleship isn't a cure-all; however I firmly believe if men and women in ministry (as well as members in our churches) were actively engaging their time in discipleship, we wouldn't be seeing so many losing their testimonies and ministries today.

## The Essentials

The essentials are the nonnegotiable elements of your disciple-making process for it to truly be considered effective discipleship. Let us review the definition of discipleship: *Discipleship is intentionally equipping believers with the Word of God through accountable relationships empowered by the Holy Spirit in order to replicate faithful followers of Christ.*

### Read the Word

The first essential element, and it is the most crucial piece, is a Bible reading plan. The Bible is the textbook. It is not some addition to all we do, but the very foundation of all we do. The Word of God is what will change our lives, and that is what we must develop a discipline for first.

We live in the most literate society and yet many are biblically illiterate—a rampant problem in our churches today. Part of the beauty of true biblical discipleship is the establishment of a regular Bible reading time. I believe it is the most crucial and essential spiritual discipline a believer can have. An article published by LifeWay stated that only 25 percent of churchgoing adults read the Bible regularly![10]

In the Old Testament, while the Israelites wandered in the wilderness for forty years, God provided manna for them. They were physically hungry and complained for food, so every morning God sent enough manna for the day. Every day for five days, they were to gather only what they needed for that day, because it would spoil overnight. On the sixth day, they were to gather double because they were to spend the Sabbath resting. This is important: They had to get up and go out and collect the manna; it didn't magically appear in their mouths. We must wake up every morning prepared to gather the spiritual sustenance needed from the Word for *that* day.

Feeding ourselves is something every follower of Christ should be able to do. We gather with other believers on Sunday mornings and depend on the minister to feed us and nourish us with the Word. We rely on prepackaged Bible studies to give us insights into what God says to us through Scripture. Do not mishear me: these things are good things. It is important to spend time with other believers in a corporate worship service. It's helpful to have someone guide us into an aspect of the Word they've studied. But if we are relying on those things to sustain us, we're resigning ourselves to the scraps of someone else's meal. The entire feast is prepared for us in the Word.

Regarding this, Leroy Eims says in his book *The Lost Art of Disciple Making,* "The problem is not that there is no spiritual food. The problem is that many Christians do not know how to get it for themselves. They are like babies in a pantry surrounded by all kinds of canned goods—meats, fruits, vegetables. But they would starve to death unless someone opened those cans for them."[11] It's our responsibility to open it and take in the nourishment.

Have you ever been anticipating a bite of something, only to learn that it is stale? I love salted caramel and chocolate. One time, I ordered a bag of salted caramel brownie crunch online and had it shipped to my house. I could not wait to rip open that bag and dig in. When I did, I couldn't have been more disappointed. It was as stale as could be! No one wants a stale snack.

For the Israelites, yesterday's manna wasn't good for today. And today's manna isn't good for tomorrow. If you are like me, you want a fresh home-cooked meal every day.

Were you ever one of those kids who did things halfway when your parents asked you to do your chores? Growing up, I was the queen of that. I would do my chores halfheartedly and my mom would always call me out on it. Unfortunately, I'm afraid I passed that trait on to one of my children. He likes to sit on the couch and watch the other one tidy up the house.

I'm afraid that's how many of us approach the Bible too. We skim a few verses someone posted on a Facebook status. If we open the Bible up, we halfway-read it or try to figure out how to write ourselves into the verses we see instead of viewing it as the centerpiece of a Christian life. A. W. Tozer said, "Nothing less than a whole Bible can make a whole Christian."[12] Regular, intentional intake of the Bible is crucial for a believer who wants to grow in the Lord. Our knowledge of the Word should lead to application and obedience to what it says.

One of the things that Jesus prays for His disciples in John 17:17 is for the Father to "sanctify them by the truth; your word is truth." We often view God's Word as restrictions and rules, when it's actually truth and freedom—truth about who God is and what He does, and the freedom that accompanies such an understanding.

I don't know about you, but when I get to heaven one day I don't want to have done this life only halfway. I want to have lived for Jesus abundantly, known His Word fully, and invested my life fervently into others for His glory. I don't want to be that girl who does things in part; I want to be a woman of God who is completely and wholeheartedly sold out for Him.

So as the leader of a D-Group, you choose what reading plan you want to do. There are endless plans to choose from. There are plans that will help you read in a historical, chronological way, plans to help you read the entire Bible in a year, and plans that take you through one topic at a time. Personally, my favorite way to read the Bible has always been chronologically. By understanding how the Old Testament fits together, it gives you a greater appreciation for the New Testament. But in the end, the best reading plan for you is the one you will actually complete.

While my husband and I were discussing the seeds of our disciple-making ministry, we got into a discussion on what we should expect of the people in our groups. I always advocated reading through the entire Bible over the course of a D-Group's life, but he would always tell me that such a requirement was unmanageable—that there's no way we could read that much *and* digest it. I told him we needed to step it up more. He'd tell me that people weren't going to want to read four or five chapters a day; I'd reply that he needed to raise the bar.

We had this discussion (or disagreement!) often.

Finally, on an eight-hour car ride to Louisiana one day, we decided to create a manageable one-year Bible reading plan that would hit every major passage in the metanarrative of Scripture in chronological order over 260 days. We believe that these are the foundational 260 passages to get a full view of God's whole story. We called the plan the F-260 (see page 199). It reads five out of seven days for fifty-two weeks (a year).

It doesn't matter what plan you choose, so long as you choose one that will help you regularly get into the Word. Maybe you focus on reading one book of the Bible a month. Maybe you sit and create your own plan with your ladies. The point is for you to choose a plan that you will all read together because this is the heart of your group and it is what everything else will be centered around.

### Memorize the Word

In a D-Group, one of the things that we focus on is hiding the Word of God in our hearts so that we have access to it at a moment's notice. One week I was working on memorizing Isaiah 41:10 and 13, which says, "Do not fear, for I am with you; do not be afraid, for I am your God. I will strengthen you; I will help you; I will hold on to you with my righteous right hand. . . . For I am the LORD your God, who holds your right hand, who says to you, 'Do not fear, I will help you.'" It was at the front of my mind all week as I was reviewing it and rehearsing it, so I began to see interactions with other people through the lens of that verse.

Suddenly I felt the need to text this verse to my friend Kim. I did, and she responded in tears—she was going through some issues with her eye and was at the doctor that morning about to undergo some tests. She said that it was exactly what she needed to be reminded of. God's Word is so reassuring in times of worry and uncertainty!

I realize that memorization doesn't come easily to everyone, but trust me when I tell you that anyone can do it. I've heard countless testimonies of women who didn't think they could remember their own phone number but are now memorization machines!

Here's the trick: start small. Memorization isn't something that only a select few are born with the ability to do, but is rather like a muscle you have to exercise in order to make it stronger. Start with one verse at a time. Print the verse off and keep it in your car to reference during the day. Write the verse on a Post-it Note and put it on your mirror or your refrigerator. This way you can see the verse and come in contact with it as you are getting ready for your day. Work on it for two weeks and then move on to the next verse right after that. See if you can recite both of them back to back. You'll find that as you flex your memorization muscles, they get stronger!

I'm not a natural-born memorization machine, so I've picked up a few other tricks along the way to help me.

First, right at the beginning of your D-Group, carve out time from each meeting to recite memory verses to each other. Start with the verse you're working on for that week and then move on to past ones that you've already memorized. This will help everyone keep each other accountable. Once you have committed more than five to memory, it will be hard to recite all of these in group time. Recite your current verse to your group and recite your other verses to yourself at least once a week.

Second, get into the habit of writing your Scripture memory verses on index cards. I like to keep mine on a ring so that I can easily flip through them and keep them from scattering all over the place in my bag.

I remember a few years ago my friend Kelli walked into our group with her memory cards and we immediately contracted the Scripture card itch: hers were perfectly laminated! It was fully in character for Kelli, though. She loves shopping at Staples and collecting office supplies, so she used the thing she loved to help her with her memorization. She went on to tell us that she bought a $20 laminating machine from Target and that she laminated them herself.

You'd better believe that we were all at Target that night! My cards are all laminated now, so they don't get tattered and torn. Also, if you put effort into making something your own, it'll stick with you in a personal way—don't be afraid to apply a little bit of creativity to your process! To this day when I pull out my laminated memory verse cards, you can see the ladies' eyes get big and they immediately contract the Scripture card itch too. They tend to follow suit very soon after.

Third, allot time for review. In my groups, we sometimes take the summer months off from memorizing new verses and use the time to review the ones we've already worked on. It's a time to be refreshed by the work we've done and to meditate on what God has spoken to us already. You might be able to memorize a hundred verses, but if you can't retain any of them, what's the point? I challenge my ladies to review for at least four weeks of the summer and then we play a game at the end. We write references on pieces of paper and stick them in a bag. Then we take turns pulling them out and seeing if we can remember. Most ladies don't like that little baggie, but it's a fun way to be accountable.

If you encounter someone who is having trouble memorizing separate verses each week, offer for them to memorize a longer passage. Sometimes I find when the verses go together they can make more sense in our brains and it can help us to retain them.

One year when we were reading through the F-260 reading plan, one lady wanted to memorize the verses attached to each week's reading and a few of us wanted to attempt a longer passage. The rest of us memorized Hebrews 11 that year. Memorizing an entire chapter made more sense to a few who had been struggling with memorization.

One more suggestion when it comes to working on memory verses is to put the passage to music, making it a song. Why is it that if we sing it we can remember it? This has been true for years and years. If you can't recall your verse week after week, try putting a tune to it.

Now, imagine coming home to find everything gone. All of your furniture, clothes, books, pictures, toys, jewelry, and electronics are missing; literally nothing exists except for the floor, walls, and ceiling.

That's exactly what happened to us in 2005 as Hurricane Katrina ripped through our city. We lived east of New Orleans at the time and had evacuated to Baton Rouge before the storm hit. We would never return to live in that house again, and we would never get the things back that the storm took from us.

Three months after the storm, we were finally able to go back to the house only to get to the threshold and realize we couldn't enter it. In addition to the eight-foot-high flood, there had been an oil spill which coated every square inch of our house. Every article of clothing. Every wedding present from eight months prior. Every picture. Every everything.

It was a harsh awakening for me to a deep, powerful truth: If I invest in those kinds of things, they can (and will) be taken away from me at some point. I may fill my house with all of the top-of-the-line gadgets and clothes and accessories, but when I get to heaven my house will be empty because I didn't store it full of things that mattered. Let us be women of the Word—who read it, memorize it, and store it in our hearts that we may live by it. Physical things may come and go, but the spiritual will last for all eternity. Robby says often that only three things are eternal: God, His Word, and the souls of men and women.

### Journal through Scripture

Every day after school, my kids and I play the High-Low game. It's just the answers to two questions: What was the highest (best) and lowest (worst) part of your day? We talk about what made an impression on them, what made them happy or sad, what confused them, and what they learned. Every time my husband returns home from a conference, I ask him the same questions. I ask those questions because I want to know what was most impactful to them. We should have the same interaction with the Word: What truth do you see about God in this passage? What things do you want to be able to remember about it? How does this passage speak to your current situation? What in this passage will effectively impact your life if you applied it?

It is incredibly easy to ensure you're doing this regularly. While there are lots of methods you can use to study Scripture, in Replicate Ministries, we call it a H.E.A.R. journal. This is a simple method to help you hear from the Lord as you get into Scripture. I've studied the Bible in various ways, all of which are wonderful, but the H.E.A.R. journal is great starting place for women new to a D-Group, as it gets them in the habit of engaging with God's Word on a daily basis.

You begin by *highlighting* a passage from your reading, *explaining* its context and what it's truly saying, *applying* it to your personal life, and *responding* to God in some way because of it.

Writing H.E.A.R. journals does two things for you. First, it helps you track the things God is teaching you through the reading of His Word. Look at this H.E.A.R. journal I wrote as I was reading through Esther in July of 2016:

> **H:** Esther 4:14: "If you keep silent at this time, relief and deliverance will come to the Jewish people from another place, but you and your father's family will be destroyed. Who knows, perhaps you have come to your royal position for such a time as this."
>
> **E:** Mordecai has requested that Esther go to the king and plead for the Jewish people. Esther is naturally fearful and knows she could die for going to the king without being summoned even though she is queen. Mordecai tells her even if she doesn't go to the king, she could die

anyway because she is a Jew. Even in the palace she wouldn't be protected.

**A:** I love this verse because it shows God's sovereignty in Esther even going to the palace in the first place. Mordecai brings up that this may be the very reason she is there. I know when I think back on my life and see all the things God did in my life or even in my kids' lives that prepared us for future events, it is so awesome. I love seeing God's hand in that way! Do we realize that what God is doing now in our lives may be preparing us for something down the road?

**R:** Lord, You know all things and You know way better than we do! I love how we see examples of this in Scripture and we can think of examples even in our own lives. Only You could plan and orchestrate those things! Thank You for Your complete control and sovereignty in our world and our individual lives!

Even now, I can see what God was teaching me about that passage in my own handwriting, and the way it impacted my life at the time. Journaling gives me a way to instantly recall the ways God was guiding and changing me through his Word in that moment. I remember the things that stuck out to me, I remember the effect it had on me, I remember the prayer I prayed as a result. But remember that the Word of God is living and active, and it will affect you differently depending on the season of life you are in.

Recently, I was reading through Esther again and found that the same verse stuck out to me upon revisiting it. Look at how the verse hit me and caused me to respond a year later:

> **H:** Esther 4:14: "If you keep silent at this time, relief and deliverance will come to the Jewish people from another place, but you and your father's house will be destroyed. Who knows, perhaps you have come to your royal position for such a time as this."

> **E:** Haman, a servant of King Ahasuerus, came up with a plot to kill all the Jewish people all because Mordecai did not bow down to him. He wanted to destroy Mordecai and all of Mordecai's people. Mordecai appeals to Queen Esther to intervene.

> **A:** What is amazing is that Mordecai fully believed relief and deliverance would come to the Jewish people. If God didn't use Esther, He would use someone else. Mordecai apparently had a strong faith and believed God's Word that He would preserve Israel. Mordecai also recognized

that Esther had been put in her position for this reason. Mordecai refused to worship anyone other than God, he recognized God's sovereignty, and he remembered God's Word. Do I ever worship anyone or anything more than God? Am I aware of God's sovereignty? Do I know God's Word well enough to remember it in difficult times? I should.

**R:** Lord, it is always encouraging to see people in your Word who remembered Your promises and trusted You would act and continue to fulfill Your Word. Mordecai seemed to be a strong man of faith and integrity. I pray that for Rig and Ryder. I want them to refuse to bow down to things of this world! I want them to see You in everything, Lord, and recognize Your sovereignty! I ask that they know Your Word so well that they always know it and can recall it in all situations!

The verse didn't change, but it impacted me differently a year later than it did the year before. I can track the way God is speaking to me by keeping a journal.

But journaling does something else in regards to discipleship: It helps you share what you're learning with those you are discipling. The cardinal rule for discipleship is that what you learn isn't only for yourself, but for those you pass it along to. For that reason, I have all of the ladies in my D-Groups journal as they read through Scripture. Then when we meet, we take time to share a H.E.A.R. journal from our week. We are all reading the same passages, but the way they impact us will be as unique as we are—and the effect Scripture has on us will be multiplied. We all take time to teach each other what God's saying to us, and through that God speaks to us over and over again.

Now, understand that I am not naturally a writer, and journaling isn't something I have always done in my life. I never kept a diary as a young girl to record my thoughts and secrets. I have always been a better speaker than a writer. However, God has given me a great love and appreciation for journaling and I can't imagine my life without it now. It is essential.

I read a book by Julie Manning called *My Heart* that reiterated what I felt about journaling. In it, she transparently and bravely shares her story of journeying through a critical diagnosis she received. She shares this about journaling: "The consistency or inconsistency of my journaling was in direct correlation to the amount of time I actually spent reading the Bible. The days and weeks when my Bible went unopened meant that I was not consistently clinging to God's truth and His promises. Thus the lies I believed in my mind spoke louder than God's Word, keeping me blindfolded in the depths of the dark wilderness."[13] Are the lies of the world speaking louder to you than God's Word? You can change that by getting into the Word until the Word gets into you!

Writing helps you remember. It makes the applications stick. It gives you a reference point to look back to. It gives you a platform to share from. If I write a journal entry, nine times out of ten, I can remember what I wrote about the following day. If I don't journal, I often forget because reading and comprehension have never been my strong suit. Journaling also helps you be intentional in not only reading but applying the Word. It aids in your reading not becoming about checking boxes.

I was recently asked to speak to a group of ministers' wives in Oklahoma. Their theme was based on Jeremiah 29:7. Guess where I went to first? My journal entries from the book of Jeremiah. I searched out what God had spoken to me when I read through parts of Jeremiah this past year. The same will be true in your D-Group. Putting in the work of journaling prepares you to be able to share God's Word with others. If you are ever asked to share a devotional or a lesson or truth from God's Word, journaling keeps you ready in season and out.

But journaling also does a third thing that strikes me in a deeply personal way. My husband and I got to have dinner with Dave Sanderson, who was on US 1549, the flight that landed in the Hudson River on January 15, 2009. He travels the globe speaking and sharing about that day in his life and all that he has learned. Something he said in that dinner gave me pause: When the plane was going down and in the chaos of the landing, he heard his mom's voice in his head saying, "You can do this." His mom wasn't there with him physically, for she had passed away. But still he heard her voice in that crazy moment. It showed me that what I invest in my boys will speak to them for years to come even if I am not here anymore.

One thing I cannot wait to pass down to my boys are my journals about what God has spoken to me through His Word. I want them to be able to have words from their momma that she received from Scripture. Can you imagine if, one day when they are faced with something seemingly insurmountable, somewhere in the back of their mind a memory comes up from something they heard me tell them God was telling me? I can think of nothing more beautiful— a mom never ceases being a mom, and God never stops being God. His Word never quits being living and active! I want to make every effort to remind them of how much I love them and of who God is. With God's grace, journaling gives me a magnificent platform to let that happen.

### Pray Together

My dear friend Audrey is a prayer warrior—the War Room, prayer-closet battle-type of warrior. She spends time every day in prayer for her family, for her friends, for the afflicted and broken, for the desperate and hopeless and whatever else is on her heart. We were talking about how to pray for someone going through something difficult. When someone tells you something that leaves you flabbergasted and you are at a loss for words, or for when you're praying for someone who has made terrible decisions, it can be hard to express your prayers and petitions.

I shared with her that I was finding it difficult to find the right words to pray for someone in my life because I was intensely discouraged. She told me that in those times she thinks of the person at the moment they accept and surrender to Christ. She talked about how it helps her attitude and her heart to envision that glorious revelation in their lives. Soon I got the chance to act on this advice.

This past year, someone close to me was in a situation that I didn't agree with or approve of. I found myself trying to balance *what* I should say and *how* I should say it. I tend to be harsh with people I expect more from, and I didn't want anything I did to damage my relationship with this person.

I began praying for her in the way Audrey advised me and immediately I felt the Lord telling me, "Kandi, your love for them must outweigh your judgment of them." This profoundly affected me because I can tend to get on my soapbox, which can be perceived as holier-than-thou—the exact opposite of what I want to do. It is so easy to be overzealous and judgmental, especially when you see others going through the same things you yourself have gone through. If you're anything like me in this, our intention is to protect them, but it can also become a pride issue, which affects our prayer life. It is not always about being right or wrong. It's about reaching others, which only comes from us truly loving others. Once I made the switch, I felt my attitude changing. It altered the way I talked about praying for the situation when I was asking for others to help me intercede. It changed the way I saw *myself.* Having a healthy attitude toward prayer dramatically changes it.

When you have a D-Group, you have a marvelous platform for prayer. It's one of the most important parts of your meetings. Each week you should be talking about any requests that need to be prayed for. Don't spend your entire time taking prayer requests, but make an effort to ask about pressing needs and then pray for them *right then.* Then, follow up with each other throughout the week to encourage one another and get updates. If additional requests come up during the week, text or email the group and ask for prayer.

As you meet over the course of a year, you will encounter and cover so many requests with each other. Anything from sickness, death, travel, work, family, children, church, divorce, drugs, sin, loss, and the list goes on. You will also celebrate praises together when God answers.

I recently realized something in my QT, and it involves prayer. You can be doing all the right things and still suffer in life. You can be in a D-group, praying, memorizing Scripture, and reading God's Word every day and that doesn't exclude you from pain or mean that God will answer your requests in the way you want. Reading in Job, I journaled on Job 1:5 which says, "Whenever a round of banqueting was over, Job would send for his children and purify them, rising early in the morning to offer burnt offerings for all of them. For Job thought, 'Perhaps my children have sinned, having cursed God in their hearts.' This was *Job's regular practice*" (emphasis mine). Job was a man of integrity who feared God and turned away from evil. He prayed to God regularly and interceded for his children, yet none of that excluded him from experiencing some of life's worst tragedies. He had a regular practice and an inner resolve to follow God. His faith was remarkable, and in all he endured he didn't blame God or sin.

Just because we are making disciples and doing everything we can to know God more and more and to obey Him, we will still go through hard and difficult situations. God may not answer our prayers in the way we want. However, we can praise Him through it. We, along with the women in our groups, can journey together and be there for each other. It's much better to journey together through the joyous times and through the difficult ones.

Bathe your ladies and your meetings in prayer, and do so with the understanding that God is the One in control. A healthy attitude and approach toward prayer is one of the foundational things to prioritize as you launch D-Groups of your own.

### Meet Weekly

Just as it is important to regularly be in the Word if you want the Word to work in your life, you should make it a priority to meet together with regularity. If you only get together once a month, you're missing a crucial part of discipleship; you can't live life with people you only see on occasion. Make each other an integral part of your lives, and your relationships with each other will only grow closer.

It helps to establish a day and time every week that is understood as your meeting time. It doesn't have to be anything fancy—it just needs to work for whatever season of life everyone is in. It can be every Wednesday morning at a coffee shop after you drop your kids off at school, or every Monday night after everyone gets off work, or every Thursday when college students have a class break. Whenever it is, you all should establish it at the start of your group so that the expectations are always consistent.

Granted, there will be times where you may have to rearrange a meeting or cancel due to vacations, holidays, or school breaks. The goal is not *meetings,* but growth—both vertical (with the Father) and horizontal (with each other). It is okay to allow flexibility so long as you are not compromising on your commitment to one another. Find a time that works and meet every week, and work out childcare if need be.

### Let Your Ladies Lead

One of my favorite parts of leading a D-Group is when I get to see the women I am discipling begin to start leading the group themselves. At the beginning, I'll facilitate discussion and keep the group on task, but as we become closer to one another and get more familiar with the process of discipleship, I'll let the other participants take turns facilitating our time together. This helps them see that they're able to do it—that leading a D-Group is not a daunting task, but rather one that overflows from the way you lead yourself.

Most women are fearful of the thought of replicating the group when we begin, but I still let them know that my expectation is that they take what we learn in the group and begin again with different people at the end of our time together. This step is important in building their confidence and their understanding that they're able to do it!

Imagine if we never taught our kids how to be independent and take care of themselves. If we never teach them basic life skills they will not ever be able to leave home and function well. They will depend on us forever, which is unhealthy for everyone involved. My mom taught me so many skills that I practice to this day. I fold towels like she does. I clean the kitchen and the bathrooms like she does. I can balance a checkbook like no other because she taught me how. I do things the way she taught me to because that's the only way I ever learned how to do them. I want the same thing for my boys. I want them to be equipped for the world.

Take, for instance, my little Ryder. He loves to do for himself. He likes to dress himself, think for himself, fix his hair by himself, and anything else you can imagine. He is very independent. One thing about my Ryder Roo is that he loves to eat—and always has. In his first moments out of the womb, his blood sugar was low; he had to immediately be given a bottle, which he sucked down so fast I was in shock. And it has been that way ever since.

He used to raid the pantry all the time, and not just *our* pantry. We would go on playdates and, when I couldn't find Ryder, I knew exactly where to look. He was in the pantry looking for applesauce and fruit snacks. He is seven now and still raids pantries! When I eventually found him climbing the shelves in our pantry like they were a ladder when he was three, we put a slider lock high up on the pantry door. But he just learned how to pull up the stepladder, climb a few steps, and unlock the pantry door. This child! He is a Gallaty through and through. All the Gallaty men love their food!

One day I decided that if he was going to eat constantly, I'd teach him how to cook. We started with oatmeal. Under my direction, he grabbed a pack out of the pantry, pulled the stepladder up to the kitchen cabinet to get a bowl, filled the bowl with the right amount of water to stir the oatmeal into, put it in the microwave on the correct settings, and let it cool after it was finished cooking so that he wouldn't burn his fingers. I took the time to teach him how to do this over and over. Now he loves to cook and bake with me all the time. He is my sous chef in the Gallaty kitchen.

The beauty of him making his own oatmeal is partly that I don't have to get up endless times a day to do it for him. He has developed the small life skill of making himself breakfast under my leadership, and now knows how to feed himself a simple meal. We do this all of the time in life. The same principles apply for discipleship. Give the ladies opportunities to lead while you assist or are nearby and they will feel more equipped than ever before when it is time to launch out on their own. By the time they are done with your D-Group, they won't have just raided everyone else's spiritual pantries, eating the nourishment someone else provided. They will know how to prepare a spiritual meal for themselves and others.

### *Provide Structure*

How you choose to structure your year together is up to you, but here is a breakdown of what the D-Group process looks like for me.

### JANUARY

In January, I lead the entire month, walking the ladies through basic techniques: how to read Scripture, how to write a H.E.A.R. journal, how to memorize Scripture.

### FEBRUARY—MARCH

During February and March we start sharing testimonies—long ones. They share for thirty to forty minutes at a time. Here are some questions I ask them to answer when sharing their testimony:

- What was your childhood like?
- Where did you grow up?
- What were you like before you met Jesus?
- How did you meet Jesus?
- How has your life been different afterwards?
- What are some spiritual markers in your life?

- What is your life verse? (You can use life
  verses as a memory verse option for that
  week too!)

Every time I ask the ladies about their experience in
D-Group, one of their most enjoyable times of the year was
hearing each woman's testimony. It is a special time and
a bonding experience. During this period, I'm still leading
the group, but the ladies are learning how to share their
life story with others. For most, it may be the first time
they have ever shared their testimony with anyone. Their
stories are incredibly rich and are worth hearing. They are
learning to lead without even realizing it.

### APRIL—AUGUST

April through August, I lead *most* of the time, continuing to strengthen our spiritual disciplines like prayer,
Scripture memory, and Bible intake.

### SEPTEMBER—DECEMBER

Then, September through December, we begin rotating
each week, allowing each lady to lead our time together.
This should be enough time for each of the ladies to partici-
pate in leading at least twice—if not more. During the first
rotation, I split the time with them. I lead the journal discussion and prayer request time and then I let them lead the
Scripture memory time and discussion of any additional
book we may be reading as a group. During the second
rotation, I have them lead the journal discussion time and
prayer request time and I lead the Scripture memory and

book discussion. Hopefully you will have time to do a third rotation and allow them to lead the entire meeting. At the end of your year together, no one can say they can't do this because they will have done it at least twice already!

If you have a group of ladies who you know are completely comfortable leading a group you may not find the need to split the time with them in order to get them used to being the leader. I had a group once that I knew were all ready and had no hesitations facilitating a group. In that case you can assign weeks for each lady to fully lead the group on their own.

Ultimately, at the end of your time together, you never want the women walking away saying, "I can't do what she just did." It is of the utmost importance they feel equipped. And even though they will be equipped, you may still have to lovingly push them out of the nest. They may be hesitant, but they will soon figure out their own ebb and flow. Make sure to encourage them: Your leading process does not have to look just like mine; this is merely a guide to help you figure out how you would like this time to look for you and your group.

Remember, the essentials are, first and foremost, a Bible reading plan, journaling a few times a week, meeting weekly, memorizing a Scripture passage each week, praying, and sharing leadership as the year goes on. These elements are the heartbeat of your process.

## The Optionals

I love incorporating extra resources during my D-Groups, but this comes with a caveat: You must never use something optional as a replacement for something essential. For instance, never read another book instead of reading Scripture. I consider the things already covered in this chapter to be essential—reading, memorizing, and journaling through the Word, praying together, and sharing leadership responsibility are indispensable parts of the discipleship process because they are each tailored to creating a disciple who makes disciples. If you have time in your schedules, though, you may consider reading some extra books together, which I love to do.

Typically, my groups read three or four books a year. If that is overwhelming, start off with one extra book. Or don't do any. Books are optional, and entirely up to you and your group dynamic. If you choose to implement a few books, start off the first few months by having everyone get into the habit of their daily quiet time. You want this established first. After the first month or so introduce the first book you will read together. Have them read a chapter a week and then discuss what you've read after journal discussion, memory verses, and prayer time.

When choosing what books to include, think about what you want to accomplish with the ladies and also take into consideration the needs of the group. Pull from different categories to give a good variety. Categories to pull from could be: discipleship, apologetics, personal growth, leadership, biblical womanhood, marriage, parenting, evangelism, doctrine, cultural engagement, and probably my favorite of all, biographies. I love reading about men and women of God who have persevered to the end and kept the faith.

In the back of this book, Appendix 1, I have listed some great books we have read over the years. There are obviously more fantastic books than those I've listed, but perhaps something in that list would strike your fancy.

As you embark on the journey of making disciples, remember that no one method is perfect. You are simply leading ladies on a journey that you, yourself, are taking too. Let everything you do be for the purpose of letting God's Word change the lives of the women you are investing in.

What follows in the rest of this book are extremely practical, behind-the-scenes tips for how to make a D-Group the most effective twelve months of your life. It is a collection of what I've learned over more than a decade of practice at making disciples. I hope that it makes you feel a bit more comfortable as you seek to make Jesus' final words your first priority.

# PART 2

# Behind the Scenes of Discipleship

# 4

# First Things First

At Replicate, we have based our ministry on the pattern that Jesus established for us when He made disciples. We believe that He's given us all of the tools we need in order to carry out the final command He gave us just before ascending to heaven: "make disciples of all nations" (Matt. 28:19).

As we talk about some of the behind-the-scenes things regarding how we recommend leading people in D-Groups, we'll be using some modern conventions that are only there to make your task easier. We're not trying to burden you with extra things; rather, we are laying out a prescriptive way to approach something that changes every time you do it. If you prepare well for a D-Group, you'll be ready to handle the day-to-day changes that come with discipling other people.

Preparing for your D-Group to begin means making sure all of your ducks are in a row administratively before your ladies arrive. I want to lay out all of the groundwork in a checklist that will help you get ready as you prepare to launch. A few of the things we will cover in this chapter are:

Invitation

Covenant/Expectations

Information Sheet

Spiritual Assessment

Materials Needed

A Reading Plan

## Invitation

Once you have prayed for potential women and gotten an overview of what your year will look like, it's time to contact the women you have been praying over so that you can extend to them an invitation. Get in touch with each woman in the way that makes the most sense for your relationship. You may want to call or text and ask if you can grab lunch and talk about starting a D-Group. Maybe you bring it up at a gathering you both already attend: Mom's Day Out, a Life Group, or a Tuesday morning spin class. However you choose to approach them about it, you may want to say something along these lines:

"Hi, _____! I have been praying for the last few months about a discipleship group that I want start in January, and God has put you on my heart. I have been praying about asking if you would join me. We will read the Bible, journal, pray for one another, and memorize Scripture for a year. Would you be interested in praying over the next few weeks to see if this is something that God leads you to do?"

You can obviously reword or create your own invitation and be as creative as you want. Once each person has had time to pray and decide whether they want to commit, you can set up a time for your whole group to meet and go over a D-Group covenant. Give them time to review and pray over the covenant so they can make their final decision and commitment.

## Covenant/Expectations

I cannot express how important it is to establish a covenant at the very beginning of your D-Group. The covenant is simply your process written down. It is everything you hope to accomplish and what you expect of everyone involved. The more your ladies know up front, the better. Give them an opportunity to pray over what you have listed as the expectations. Once they say they are in, have them sign the covenant and turn it in to you and keep them in a file.

Ladies often contact me once they have started their own groups with questions of how to navigate issues like someone not being on board, someone not wanting to commit to the reading plan, or not contributing to the group discussion. I first ask whether they signed a covenant. Almost always, the answer is no. The beauty of the covenant is that when issues like these come up (and they will), you can pull it out and address the issues at hand by graciously reminding her of what she agreed to at the beginning. Remind her that you all signed a covenant and see if there is anything you can do to help her get back on track.

The covenant is not a fix-all by any means. You will still encounter issues within the group due to sin, or laziness, or struggles in general. However, a covenant can greatly minimize some of those issues because it will fully state what is expected of each person before the group even starts.

If you find yourself in the middle of a group right now and you didn't make a covenant, you can easily create one. Have the ladies go over it and use this as a time of recommitment. I did this in my eighteen-month group. Since we were meeting for so long, at the start of the last six months, I had them resign the covenant. I wanted them to recommit and finish strong.

As you are thinking through putting together a covenant, consider including things like:

- What Bible reading plan will you use?
- How many times will you journal each week?
- How many verses will you memorize per week?
- How long will your group meet?
- Will you read extra books?
- What are your expectations for attendance?

In Appendix 2 there are a couple of examples of covenants for you to look over. The point is not to strap someone down with legalism, but to establish every expectation up front so that you can keep each other accountable as you grow.

## Information Sheet

On your first meeting, you will be buzzing with excitement to begin getting to know each other better. The ladies in your group will be three or four of your closest companions over the next year. I've found that having a short questionnaire is helpful in knitting your group closer together.

This is by no means mandatory, but it's a fun way to begin your first meeting. You get to read each other's responses and hold on to them to serve as points of reference throughout the year. You can ask any questions you want: When is your birthday/anniversary? What is your favorite place to go out to eat? Where do you love shopping? Get specific. Get creative. This is entirely to help you get to know each other better.

I make each lady a copy of everyone's sheet. This way we all have access to the answers. I can't tell you how many times we look at these sheets during our year together. If you celebrate birthdays and want to give a gift to the birthday girl, you have an easy point of reference to know everything from her favorite candy bar to what she likes to do when she's stressed out.

In addition to getting to know what sorts of things each lady likes, you can also use the questionnaire to get a brief spiritual background. We call these Spiritual Journey Inventories. A Spiritual Journey Inventory might look like this:

> After coming to the Lord, I finally understood _____.
>
> The closest I have felt to God in my life was _____.
>
> The farthest I felt from God was _____.
>
> If I could change one incident in my life it would be _____.
>
> One incident in my life that I would never change would be _____.
>
> The turning point in my relationship with God was _____.

Any questions that you can use to get to know the ladies is helpful.

I leave you with one more suggestion to get to know one another better. In my groups, a few months after we begin meeting, I like to play a game called "Pull a Question Out of the Bag." Original, isn't it? We go somewhere we don't usually, meet at a time we don't usually get together, and take turns pulling questions out of a bag and answering them. These are not overly spiritual questions, they're questions like, "If you could have been born at any other time, when would it be and why?" and "What is the most adventurous thing you have ever done?" These are just fun questions that give insight into each lady. Feel free to get creative when getting to know your ladies.

## Spiritual Assessment

Because each of you will likely have different spiritual backgrounds, it may be helpful for you to have each of your ladies fill out a spiritual assessment. The one I recommend is from *DiscipleMakers International* entitled "Self-Assessment Questionnaire: Christian Fundamentals." It asks twenty-seven questions that deal with assurance of salvation, what it means to be a new creation in Christ, and other foundational questions. Have the group answer these privately for only you to see. You may want to read over their responses to see if there are any issues you need to address during your year together. It may provide insight as to what spiritual truths you would like to teach them or what books you want to read together.

Sometimes these answers could be bothersome. If you think a one-on-one meeting is necessary, feel the freedom to do so. You are the leader of the group, and you are there to serve the ladies in it. Take an opportunity at the beginning of your D-Group to know where each woman stands spiritually, and it will help you serve and minister to each of them better.

## Materials Needed

There are materials that you need to ensure both you and your group members have on hand. Most important, they need a Bible! I strongly encourage a study Bible with study notes at the bottom. Since everyone is reading at home, there will definitely be times they don't understand something. If they are reading on their own and don't have you around to answer a question for them, they will be able to glance right there at the notes and hopefully gain insight. My ladies will often text me with questions about something they are confused about and my first go-to source, if I don't know the answer offhand, is my study Bible. I also have a study Bible app on my phone for quick reference at any time. (Blue Letter Bible has an excellent app for your electronic devices.)

Because one of the things we emphasize in D-Groups is journaling, everyone will need something to write in. This can be a physical journal, an Evernote folder, or anything that lets you store thoughts in an easy-to-access way. Replicate Ministries has actually released a free app that is designed to make this easier; it is available for both iPhone and Android users. It allows you to set up a group (like your D-Group), read Scripture, and write H.E.A.R. journals all in one place. Then, because you are a part of a group, the rest of the members can see the things you've written. This will help you stay accountable to complete the reading and journaling, and will help you use what you're learning to minister to others. If you read an entry and are particularly challenged or encouraged, you can leave a little comment below the journal entry.

The Replicate App also lets you enter in prayer requests and take Scripture memory quizzes for the verses included in the F-260.

Also, it may be helpful for you to provide tools to help memorize Scripture. Index cards have been used for years for a reason: because they work! Write the reference on the front and then the verse on the back and you have a built-in system to learn and quiz yourself. There are a number of apps available for this, like Fighter Verses. You can do research and use the method that is most helpful to you.

## A Reading Plan

Finally, make sure everyone has access to the reading plan you will be using. Whether it's available online or you print it out and hand it to them, make sure they have it as soon as possible.

As you prepare to launch a D-Group, remember that all of this is simply for the purpose of facilitating spiritual growth. You want your ladies to develop into strong women of God, so all of your actions and preparations should be done with that end in mind.

# Ready, Set, Go

You've done all of the preparation. You've invited the women you are going to disciple. You've gathered all of the materials you need. Now comes the moment of truth: When do you start?

There's no hard-and-fast rule about this. When it comes down to it, the perfect start time is the one that works best for you. But there are two times that seem to work best for most people: January and August/September. This semester type of schedule works well for high school students, college students, parents whose children are in school, church staff members, and so on.

But remember, these are just suggestions. Sometimes an unexpected time frame works just fine. For example, I was meeting with a group of ladies a few years ago, one of whom was pregnant. She was due to have her baby toward the end of December. Instead of starting her new group in January, she waited until April—after she would have adjusted (as much as you can!) to being a new mother. Her group met from April to April of the following year and it totally worked.

Once you determine a start date, pick a day or night of the week that works for each of your women. Our church allows groups to meet all over campus on Wednesday nights, so many use that time (when the kids are able to go to Wednesday night activites) to meet. It may be that you choose to meet every Thursday for lunch at a favorite local restaurant or Saturday during brunch at a coffee shop. Sometimes my groups switch up our meeting place and decide to grab coffee or dessert after the kiddos are in bed for the night.

The main thing is to have a regular meeting time and place each week. If childcare is a factor for some of the women in your group, work together to figure out how to best navigate it. Maybe you choose to meet while your kids are in school or in a Mother's Day Out program. Maybe you are discipling other moms from the school your kids go to, and you decide to meet after you drop off your kids. I have met everywhere from Wednesday nights at the church, to Tuesdays right after lunch, to Thursday afternoons at the coffee shop each week, and countless other times and places in between. If someone's work schedule is a factor, plan to meet before the day begins for them, or during a regular meal break they may have in their shift, or any evening that works for all the members of the group outside of their work hours.

After you pick your start date all you need to do is proceed!

## Managing Your Time Together

Once I had a conversation with a woman whose biggest problem with her D-Group was that they simply couldn't wrap it up in time. Most groups meet for between an hour and an hour and a half a week; hers was consistently going longer than two hours. Women like to talk, but we need to be respectful of everyone's time. It's up to you as the leader to keep everyone on time. Remember to manage your time or it will manage you. Below are two sample guides to help you come up with a format for your time together.

If you are meeting for 1 hour:

- 5 minutes—chat about the week to catch up and then open in prayer
- 5 minutes—accountability (recite your memory verses to one another, etc.)
- 10 minutes—discuss books you may be reading together, share testimonies, etc.
- 30 minutes—share journal entries from that week
- 10 minutes—summarize, apply anything you want, talk about any pressing prayer requests, and close in prayer

Suggestion: If you are in the season of sharing testimonies and you are limited on time due to only meeting for an hour, you can take up some of the time allotted for journal entry discussion. If you post journals to an app, have everyone read them on the app those weeks instead of discussing

them in group. You can also have everyone text out their
journal that week.

Another alternative is to have everyone over one night
and share testimonies together all in one night. That could
get lengthy but is totally doable. You could also go away on
an overnight retreat to share your stories with one another.
I would do this in a private setting because sometimes this
can be emotional for women and you may not want to be at
a crowded restaurant while sharing some of these stories.
Again, that is totally up to you and these are merely suggestions to help you think through how you would best like to
do this.

If you are meeting for 1½ hours:

- 15 minutes—chat about the week to
  catch up and then open in prayer
- 5 minutes—accountability (recite memory verses to one another, etc.)
- 20 minutes—discuss books you may be
  reading, share testimonies, etc.
- 40 minutes—share journal entries from
  that week
- 10 minutes—summarize, apply anything you want, talk about any pressing
  prayer requests, and close in prayer

Remember, these are only suggestions to help you see
how to divide your time together. Occasionally, based on the
needs of your group, you may get off track. That's fine. Don't
be so closed-fisted about managing your group's schedule

that you choke out the Holy Spirit. You want to be sensitive to your group's needs and at the same time hear what God is speaking to them each week in their reading. Emphasize personal responsibility and encourage accountability, and many of these problems will resolve.

When I teach and discuss certain topics that may be confusing in Scripture, I do it during the time of journal entry sharing or book discussion. That isn't an every-week thing. It's only when I feel in my heart further explanation could be helpful. For example, a younger believer might find topics like the tabernacle, its elements, the Feasts, or the Divided Kingdom as hard things to wrap her mind around, so I'd make it a point to be sensitive to the leading of the Holy Spirit.

It is also helpful on occasion to study a passage together in your meeting time. Read it fresh together and look for truths about God. You can discuss the passage and what you discover and learn from it. This could be insightful especially for those who may be new to reading and studying the Bible.

Still, having something of a schedule helps as you instill the process of replication into each of your ladies. It's easier to replicate something specific than it is to throw them in and expect them to wing it. Soon, the "schedule" will be second nature to you and you'll find it easy to be a bit more flexible.

# 6

# Maturity Matters

Taking ladies through a D-Group is like planting a seed. First, it is going to grow a woman who is both a disciple and a disciple-maker. It is also going to produce a woman who displays the specific fruit that discipleship produces in our lives. Let's take a look at both of these outcomes.

## The Goals of a D-Group

Generally speaking, you should have two goals for the women in your D-Group: spiritual growth and replication. You want your ladies to grow spiritually and then turn around to help other women grow spiritually too. The whole point of being a disciple is to follow after Christ and become more like Him. We do this first by getting into the Word. This helps us know God better. When we get to know God better, we love Him more because of what we learn about Him. The more we love Him, the more we obey Him. As we obey God, He reveals Himself more to us, causing us to know Him better and the whole process to start over.

In his book *Growing Up*, Robby gives a visual of this cycle. It is a triangle with the top as "Know God" which leads to "Love God" and then "Obey God." The more you know Him, the more you will love Him, and the more you love Him, the more you will want to obey Him. Think of it like this: The more *disciplined* you are leads to *desire* which leads to *demonstration* and *devotion* to God.

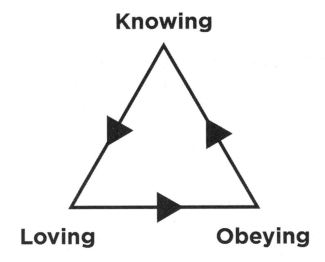

**Knowing**

**Loving**           **Obeying**

The more this cycle grows in your life, the more disciplined you will be in your walk with Him. It's a growth pattern that will continue to repeat in your life. A D-Group will give you a team of women all helping one another in their pursuit of a growing relationship with God.

Because the first step is to know God better, developing biblical literacy and a biblical worldview are the first two things you should shoot for. These two things will help you meet your goal of spiritual growth like none other. As you journey along and read the Word regularly, using it to guide discussion about life issues week in and week out, you begin to become more literate of the Bible and you develop a lens through which you view the things you are dealing with. You begin to see things as God sees them and make decisions as He would.

As I write this, I am reminded of a particular time in a D-Group when I saw this happen. We were on Week Eleven of the F-260, reading about the Exodus of the Israelites and their time in the wilderness. We had all journaled on different verses that week, so most of our time was spent discussing the Israelites' complaints, Moses' burden during all of these years, the lack of support he and Aaron received, the frustration Moses experienced, and how the people never seemed happy or content. We left that meeting thinking about how we act the same way today. We addressed the frequent discontent we feel in various aspects of our lives, even when God has provided us with everything we need. We each left that meeting profoundly grateful for what we had and for what God had done in our lives.

Al Mohler, president of The Southern Baptist Theological Seminary, says, "The tragedy that evangelicals have lost the art of biblical discernment must be traced to a disastrous loss of biblical knowledge. Discernment cannot survive without doctrine."[14] In order for us to be able to discern things in this life we must know God's Word more and more. We must be educated continuously in the only thing that can change us—and that is His Word.

Not only should we become educated about who God is and who we are in light of that, we should also see D-Groups as a way to become equipped—another part of our goal of spiritual growth. So many life circumstances arise in a year's time. We might be equipped in small ways, like learning how to pray through situations with difficult neighbors. We might become equipped in big ways, like how to minister to loved ones after a family member dies. We become prepared to do these things well because we deal with them together, under the direction of the Holy Spirit.

You will also be equipped with the wisdom that accompanies a deep understanding of God's Word. You should learn how to make wise choices and be a mature Christian. Of course, this will not entirely eliminate the existence of bad choices or sin in your life, but a D-Group helps you and your ladies understand how to healthily deal with those things when they arise.

In addition to becoming equipped to share your life and make wise and mature choices, D-Groups train you and your ladies how to manage and prioritize your time—another indicator of spiritual growth. Time management isn't as easy for some as others, which is okay. It can be learned together.

Occasionally a woman will come to me and say she is having a hard time fitting it all in. If that happens, I sit down with her and try to find ways to help her. For example, years ago, I was sitting down with a woman having a hard time fitting in her quiet time. We went through a typical day for her and tried to find the right time in her schedule that would work for a regular intentional time with Jesus. I began to suggest some options.

Our conversation went like this:

> "What about waking up early before the kids get up to do your quiet time?"

> "Well, that's when I work out. If I don't do it then, it won't get done."

> "Okay, what about your lunch break?"

> "I only get about thirty minutes for lunch at work, and I just don't have time to do that and the other things I need to do."

> "What about waiting in the car line for drop-off or pick-up? Can you listen to the Bible in the car?"

> "Well, typically I am putting on my make-up in carline."

> "Okay, what does your night look like? Can you read after you put the kids to bed?"

> "After I put the kids to bed, I sit down with my husband and we watch a few hours of TV together."

I thought, *Bingo!* But instead of saying that, I said, "I see. Well, watching TV and spending time with our hubbies is important. My husband and I watch a show together at night as well. But do you think you can take thirty minutes of your two hours to do your quiet time if you can't find another time to do it?"

The fact is that I don't believe spending time in the Word was a priority to her at that point. And maybe she didn't realize that before we had that conversation. Everything else in her life was getting done, but Scripture was taking a back seat. The Lord has given us a twenty-four-hour day, so we should be able to carve out time to spend with Him. We have to be able to manage our time and take care of ourselves.

I regularly work out, put my makeup on, spend time with my husband and kids, and do all of the things that she mentioned, but I don't do it at the expense of my time with the Lord. Don't take for granted that all your ladies have a regular quiet time. It takes practice and intentionality to develop one. You may need to spend some time with them at the beginning talking about time management and priorities. You will help them develop this discipline from which all other disciplines will flow.

As I've said before, we have to manage our time or our time will manage us. Everyone has busy days and seasons of life. Things may have to be adjusted or times may have to change, but it can be done. It may take listening to the Bible in her car, listening while she folds laundry or cleans the kitchen or gets in a workout, or getting up earlier than she usually does. Whatever it takes, a major goal of your D-Group should be helping these women manage their time in a way that gives *God* the priority in their lives.

I've said before that I wake up one hour before my kids do every day (except Saturday, which is my day to sleep in!) in order to spend time in the Word, journal, and pray. I can't live without this time. I look forward to it every morning. I know me and I am the most productive during the morning hours. But if I didn't make it a priority early on, I never would have developed the habit—I'd be letting my time manage me instead. If you are a night owl, your time in the Word may be at night. If you spend hours in the car for work or on a plane, your time may be then. Plan a time, put it on your calendar if you have to, and prioritize your meeting with the Lord! You will not be sorry!

The second goal of a D-Group should be *replication*, or in other words, *learning to lead*. As you lead and give the ladies opportunities to lead as well, you are helping them to establish both the ability to lead a D-Group and practice leadership in their lives. You do this in small steps: first, by allowing them to share their testimony. This helps them practice taking ownership of their faith. When women share their testimonies, they are demonstrating leadership without even realizing it. They are leading the group just by opening their mouth and sharing about what God has done in their lives. Ultimately, as I've mentioned (I don't know that I can mention it enough!) you want to empower them to take what they've learned and replicate it in other women whom they will teach to lead others as well.

Educating, equipping, and empowering ladies to walk with God and lead well are the goals of a discipler. And if your group commits to these things together before the

Lord, overall life transformation should be the end result. If nothing else, you will have taught them and modeled for them how to have an intentional quality time with the Lord through the reading and journaling of His Word. When all else fails they will know where to go to hear from God.

## Fruit of a D-Group

As you become a disciple-maker who makes more disciple-makers, the first thing that you'll notice about yourself is that you've grown in one type of fruit: *knowledge of God*, which fuels your walk with Him. Just knowing things about Him isn't enough though; information alone doesn't guarantee transformation. Another type of fruit that a D-Group bears is that of *life change*. D-Group gives you space to act upon the things you learn, which will in turn allow you to take it out of the group and into your everyday life.

This is a process we call *sanctification*: it is you being continually transformed into the image of Christ. God, through the Spirit inside of you, changes you. Learning and obeying His Word is the first step in that process. Before long, the Word becomes something you thirst for, without which you can't survive. Once you establish a connection with your Maker and learn the way He designed you to live, anything else feels like a cheap forgery.

But D-Groups are not merely a means to personal benefit; they also cultivate another kind of fruit: *unity*, unlike anything you've seen before. You are suddenly living side by side with other like-minded believers. When you are all focused on something so much bigger than yourselves, conflict seems to fade into the background and be replaced by what you're learning of Jesus' character by studying His Word.

While you are walking with these women, you will hear of all kinds of outer conflict they are trying to navigate, perhaps with a difficult family member or workplace acquaintance.

Not too long ago it was nearing Thanksgiving and everyone in my group had family coming into town. Numerous ladies had members of their families who were lost and definitely not serving the Lord, and sometimes those family members would poke fun or just be hard to deal with. As we sat around asking for prayer for each situation, we determined to be a light to our family members even if they were difficult. We used each other to call one another to action. The unity we felt was soon overflowing to the people outside of our group in our everyday lives. When you are praying for someone and trying to show them the light and love of Christ, it is hard to be at odds with them. Not only will you notice growth and unity in your life, but in the lives of those you love and care for as well.

When unity begins flowing to the people around us, it is generally accompanied by *service*: the next fruit of a D-Group. You will spend time serving one another and looking after each other's needs; soon, you'll find that service is something that comes naturally to you. It doesn't always look the same for each individual, but you will find yourself asking people how you can help them, what parts of their burdens you can shoulder, and what things they need to help them make it through the week. Sometimes it's only through intentionally sharing your life with a few that you learn how to share it with many.

The final fruit, and the ultimate goal of discipleship, is *replication*: making sure the disciple-making journey continues. If the disciples hadn't taken Jesus' command seriously, none of us would be here now having this conversation about the Messiah they served. Having someone take what was invested and taught to them and turn around and invest that into someone else is what discipleship is all about.

# Elements of an Effective D-Group

If a business wants to know how healthy it is, it's not exactly rocket science. It can look at the money in versus money out, the number of new locations opened, how much its profits increased, and how many employees it hired, for starters. You can pick up a book on how to measure business growth at any bookstore across the country.

So how do we measure our effectiveness when making disciples? Is it all about numbers? If it were about numbers, we should be cramming our groups full of women and launching them as quickly as possible, don't you think?

Instead of looking for sheer volume, we try to probe a bit deeper. Remember, the goal of discipleship is to make *faithful* followers of Christ. That means we're looking for something that is more qualitative than quantitative. We can't measure it just by looking at numbers.

For this reason, we've come up with a useful acronym to help you gauge the spiritual health of the women you are discipling (and also your D-Groups). You want to look for the MARCS of a disciple: they should be Missional, Accountable, Reproducible, Communal, and Scriptural. Let's take a look at what each of these MARCS entails.

## Missional

When Christ departed from earth, He told the disciples in Acts 1:8: "But you will receive power when the Holy Spirit has come on you, and you will be my witnesses in Jerusalem, in all Judea and Samaria, and to the end of the earth." It was His plan that we lead a lifestyle of mission—that no matter where we go, we are His witnesses. Every facet of our lives should reflect the risen King. A D-Group is the perfect context to get the hang of missional living so that it can overflow into the world around you.

Years ago when my boys were tiny toddlers, I had a desire to take my discipleship group on a mission trip to the Dominican Republic, where I've worked with sex trafficking safe houses through a local ministry there. I wanted my ladies to experience what it was like to serve in another country and get a richer perspective of life beyond our own city and state.

As I brought up the topic with Robby, he voiced his support but told me he needed me at home during this season. He was finishing his doctorate and pastoring a growing church while fathering two young boys. I told my ladies

what I had been considering and they agreed that the tim-
ing wasn't perfect—they all had growing children and busy
schedules too. A trip out of the country just wasn't ideal at
that moment. In hindsight, I am so glad I didn't push Robby
to let me go on a trip. He ended up having a pacemaker put
in during this time in our lives. I could have pushed and
schemed to get him to let me go on the trip, which would
have been completely wrong. Over the years, I have learned
to not only trust my husband when he tells me something
but to trust the Lord through my husband.

So we started brainstorming how to be missional without going to the "utmost parts." I went to the missions office
at our church and asked them for every missionary card of
every missionary we supported as a church. I got six cop-
ies of the cards—one for each of us in the group. I took the
cards, punched a hole in the upper left corner, and fastened
them with a ring. I handed these "Missionary Prayer Rings"
out at the next meeting, letting my ladies know we were
going to be praying for a missionary a day when we do our
quiet time.

Though I didn't know many of the people on the cards,
they each had the location they were serving, what they were
doing there, and what specific things they had requested
people pray for. We began to pray for this group regularly,
and what surprised me the most was the work that the Lord
did on each of our hearts. We began to feel knitted together
with these missionaries!

One young woman in particular who we had been praying for was going through a challenging time, as she was in a

difficult location by herself and was going through intense spiritual warfare. A team from our church happened to be going to visit her at this time, so we asked them to let her know we were praying on her behalf. She was so blown away that a group of six ladies across the world was praying for her each week. It opened up a way for us to receive emails from her and begin sending her little gifts and care packages. We really felt like we began to know her through our prayer time for her.

It's a misconception to think that living missionally means you need to go overseas. That is definitely a part of it, but what it means more accurately is that your perspective of your everyday life needs to shift. You view things from a kingdom perspective: the people around you are not just outer shells, they are embodied souls in need of a Savior. The things you face are not products of a random universe, but are events that mold you into the person God wants you to be. Living on mission means that wherever you are, you are viewing those around you differently than you did before you were adopted into God's Kingdom.

Ever since the year we made those missionary prayer rings, I've made it a regular practice to hand them out to the ladies in my D-Groups. I encourage my ladies to reach out to the people they are praying for and encourage them, let them know they are praying, and ask what they can do to help. I started putting a family photo of each lady's family in the missionary prayer rings to remind us that our families are missionaries everywhere we go. I love doing the same thing with our staff directory so that we can pray for the families of the people serving our church. You can also book ring your Christmas cards and pray for those family and friends throughout the year.

As you spend your time praying for people serving overseas and at your church, you'll find that you begin looking for ways to serve people outside those circles. Perhaps you want to take your D-Group to visit the local nursing home, make cookies for police officers or firefighters, make care packages for local teachers, adopt an underprivileged family at Christmas, or volunteer at a food shelter down the street. Your church also, most likely, has numerous opportunities for you to serve as a family for outreach. The number of ways you can be intentional with the people around you is almost endless.

Finally, the easiest way to live on mission is to be constantly praying for and seeking opportunities to share your faith. Because many D-Groups meet in public places, often they don't even have to look for these opportunities, because inevitably someone comes up and is curious about what they are doing. I've heard stories of ladies meeting in coffee shops at the same time every week who eventually get asked by the baristas they see all the time just what is going on. That is automatically a way to share what the Lord is doing: they simply explain that they have some ladies who meet every week with the intention of becoming more Christlike. Whether it's building a relationship with your local barista, your hairstylist, a new friend at the gym, your neighbor down the street, some coworkers, or a woman who shares the same hobby as you, there are so many creative ways that you can be missional in your daily life!

## Accountable

If you think about it, we are accountable to multiple people and even entities. If you are married, you are accountable to your spouse. When you were a child, you were accountable to your parents. We are all subject to laws of our land and accountable to our government.

Not too long ago, I am sad to say, I was pulled over for speeding. We had just moved to a new area, and I wasn't aware of the speed limits along that particular highway. The road was curvy and hilly, and for whatever reason my speed had completely gotten away from me.

When I saw the officer behind me, my first thought was that he needed to pass me to go catch someone ahead of me. When I pulled off to the side, I realized he wasn't passing me, he was getting over behind me! I can't tell you the last time I was pulled over.

The officer walked up to the window and asked me for my driver's license, registration, and insurance. Meanwhile, Rig, from the back seat, asked the officer if we were on "LivePD"—a show that follows police officers with cameras to see situations and people they pull over. We weren't, thank goodness! I was so embarrassed.

While he called in all my info and wrote me a ticket, the boys were losing their minds with laughter in the back seat. Mommy had gotten pulled over! They were chanting,

"Call Daddy, call Daddy!" They laughed about it the whole time. The officer walked back to the window to hand me the ticket, at which point Rig began asking him every question under the sun. The commotion was comical in hindsight—Rig being riled up, Ryder feeding off of Rig's energy, the officer trying to explain over the commotion what my next steps were, and me, melting from embarrassment, in the front seat. The officer actually asked me how many kids I had in the car with me. I said, "Only two." As he walked off, Rig said to him, "Sir, thank you for your service, Sir." This boy! Needless to say, we called Daddy right after.

As a citizen of my city, I am accountable to the laws, even if I am not aware of all of them. It's part of citizenship. This officer was holding me accountable to the speed limit laws. Accountability may not always be fun, but it's a built-in system designed to keep us safe. Accountability in discipleship works the same way. The idea sounds great, but when you are the one who is being asked to pick up the slack you're leaving, it can be stressful. That's okay. Accountability keeps us honest and on track.

Ecclesiastes 4:9–12 says, "Two are better than one because they have a good reward for their efforts. For if either falls, his companion can lift him up; but pity the one who falls without another to lift him up. Also, if two lie down together, they can keep warm; but how can one person alone keep warm? And if someone overpowers one person, two can resist him. A cord of three strands is not easily broken." We get to live this kind of accountability out in D-Groups.

First, you need accountability in the *disciplines* you are accomplishing each week. For instance, we read our Bible daily, memorize our verse weekly, and journal consistently. If I never asked my group if they are following through on these, I would never know what God is doing in their lives or if they are experiencing spiritual growth. By checking in with them every time we get together, not only do I get to see this progress, but we keep each other in check and give them the motivation they need to continue on.

The beautiful thing about accountability is that it often keeps you from having to be the bad guy and address someone who might be wandering, struggling, or slacking off. When we come to group and quote our memory verse to each other, and we get to a person who, for some reason, did not memorize theirs that week, I don't have to say a word. Once we get to them, their lack of preparation speaks loud and clear. They will likely have a rude awakening like I did when I got pulled over for speeding and will step it up next week. I won't have to say a word because the group accountability did it for me. And believe me, I have learned to slow down and keep a close watch on my speed now.

On a side note, after I received the ticket for speeding, I had to go to court. I wanted it removed from my record and to do that, you have to appear before the judge. I learned that since it was my first ticket, I could plead guilty and go to a four-hour traffic school. The last thing I had time to do was to sit in a four-hour traffic class, but this was the only option. I went to court and I will never forget it. I was sitting in a room full of people. No one was talking to each other, we were just all waiting. The judge came in and we all rose. He called us up in groups of ten. We were in a single-file line as we approached the microphone. I was a nervous wreck because I knew I had to speak into this microphone, that I was guilty.

In that moment, all I could think of is the judgment seat of Christ! In my head and heart, I knew I was not guilty in God's divine court because Jesus had saved me and paid my penalty. But in that moment, I was guilty of speeding. I was thinking to myself, *I can't believe I have to say I am guilty of something.* It was truly bothering me. And there I was when my turn finally came, standing behind the microphone. He asked my name and asked guilty or not guilty? I sheepishly said, "Guilty." He said, "Traffic school," and I turned and walked out.

I was so glad this was over, but even more, I was so incredibly thankful that when Christ forgave, redeemed, and restored me, He didn't put a stipulation on it. He didn't assign me to a class or a seminar to have my record wiped clean. He canceled the debt because He paid it! My record is clean and I stand in His righteousness not my own. Praise Him!

Accountability around spiritual disciplines isn't the only form of accountability in a D-Group, but it tends to be the easier of the two. The other form of accountability the D-Group provides is *sin* accountability. Listen. It is difficult to ask people about specific sins they are struggling with, but if you have a heart for the women you disciple, your love for them will compel you to make sure they are staying on the rails. You as the leader may have to ask the tough questions which may reveal a secret sin that needs to be addressed. I have had this occur a few times in a few different ways.

One time a woman in my group came to me about a relationship she had been in that was sinful. She had been dating a married man for a few months, right after our D-Group began. No one knew or even had a clue. She and I went to lunch one day, just the two of us, and she confessed this to me through many tears and much heartbreak. The relationship was over and she was in an emotional whirlwind with it all. I cried with her, spoke truth to her, and encouraged her to go home and confess to the Lord, repent, and refrain from dating this man. We kept this private from the group and just between us at that point.

Four months went by and she had begun dating a new guy (which she bravely told the group about this time around). I was on vacation for my husband's sabbatical and I just got this gut feeling that I needed to ask her about her relationship. I wanted to see if she was honoring the Lord or if she was submitting to self and sin. I texted her about the relationship and after she said they were still dating, I asked the tough question: "Are you being intimate with him?" She was honest and said she was. I told her we had to meet as soon as I got back from vacation.

I had time to pray and prepare what I would say to her as we sat across my dining table. When we sat down, I told her how much I loved her and how much I wanted to see what all God wanted to do in her life. However, she could not continue in this D-Group with habitual sin in her life. What makes it more difficult is this particular woman had lost a child a year and a half before this. All of the ladies in our group rallied around her and just wanted to love her through this most difficult and grievous time. As I sat across from her in tears, I told her I could not imagine what she had gone through, but as hard as her life had been with the loss of her child, I couldn't let this sin go unaddressed. I wouldn't be her true friend if I didn't point her to the Lord and ask her to follow Him in this area of her life.

She had signed a covenant with our group and given me the liberty to speak into her life (one of the great things about signing a covenant up front). Her tragedy didn't justify her being able to live in sin. We both cried that day and once again, I gave her truth, love, and Scripture. I told her that no other sin so clearly affects the body as sexual sin. I told her God was not going to bless that relationship, and that I didn't want to see her have to experience the consequences of that kind of sin. I told her how much I believed God wanted to do great things in her life, but me wanting it for her wasn't enough. She needed to be willing to pursue a life of holiness for the Lord and for herself.

I asked her to pray about a few things as she left. First, if she was to remain in our group she needed to come and confess what was going on to the group. It was now time to up the accountability to the group level. These ladies that were journeying with her had the right to know what was going on in her life in order to help her. Second, if she came and confessed to the group and remained in the group, she needed to abstain from sexual intercourse for the rest of our time together. All in all, I was asking her to commit to group transparency and willingness to follow God instead of habitual sin. If she couldn't do those two things—two things she originally covenanted to do at the start—then she couldn't come back to the group.

To this day, that has been the hardest situation I have been in as a disciple-maker. As she left that day, I prayed that the Lord would use what I had shared with her and the Scriptures I had shared to speak life to her. Frankly, I also prayed I had not butchered this! After a week went by she decided not to come back to us. I was saddened but I kept moving forward, knowing this was the right thing to do. I went back to our group and told them our friend had some sin in her life which at that point she was not ready to confess and leave behind, and therefore she wouldn't be continuing on with us. I encouraged them to reach out and let her know how much they loved her.

A few months went by and I got a text from her wanting to meet for lunch. We met and chatted for a bit, and then she said to me, "The biggest mistake I made was not coming back to D-Group." She cried and told me how God was working in her life and how He had been dealing with her about what wise counsel is and how she needed it in her life. She shared with me multiple Scriptures God had given her and even a song that had been really speaking to her.

God had shown her Proverbs 12:15, which says, "A fool's way is right in his own eyes, but whoever listens to counsel is wise." She also shared Proverbs 11:14, which says,

"Without guidance, a people will fall, but with many counselors there is deliverance." The song that really spoke to her was "No Man Is an Island" by Tenth Avenue North. The chorus to that song says, "No man is an island, we can be found, no man is an island, let your guard down. You don't have to fight me, I am for you. We're not meant to live this life alone."[15] How true are these words! We aren't meant to live this life alone!

The devil wants nothing more than to keep us in isolation. If he can get us to keep our areas of struggle silent, he wins. But as soon as you speak it out loud, he loses power. We have to get to a place where we are transparent with a few trusted people in order to have victory over sin and strongholds in our lives. If we keep it private and secret, we continue to sin. Share it and be transparent, and it will begin to lose its hold on you.

A rule of thumb is: If you feel the need to do it in secret, that's an indication you don't need to be doing it. You should be able to freely share your life without having something to hide. Hiding is unhealthy and oftentimes harmful. If you feel the need to conceal, you really need to reveal what is going on.

After our lunch, she asked if she could come back to the group. I happily agreed. We journeyed together for another few months before it became apparent, once again, that this just wasn't the time or season for this group in her life. I started noticing that her tragic loss and desperate coping measures meant she was in need of greater counseling than I could give her. Don't get me wrong. It wasn't as if she was "too much" for us. It was *us* not being enough for what *she* really needed in that season. Sometimes as a leader, you need to be able to swallow your pride and push people to someone who is better trained than you are.

After all, discipleship is not meant to be a counseling session. I don't want that to sound harsh but you, as a leader, will need to be aware of needs beyond your ability and point those ladies to someone who can help them. You won't always have circumstances that are this extreme; nevertheless, you will face a multitude of complex situations over the years. You have to pray and discern how the Lord wants you to handle each one. Pray over each and every situation, look to Jesus for wisdom, and do everything you can to foster a spirit of accountability among those in your D-Group.

On another occasion, I had a lady confess something the Lord had convicted her of. On this day we happened to be meeting to discuss her upcoming turn to lead our group. We were meeting for lunch, and as we met up in the parking lot to walk into the building, I asked her a question that I thought was just that, a simple question. I had no idea the Lord would use it to confirm to her that she needed to share with me about something private in her life. I said to her, "How are you feeling? I feel like you have really been struggling with these bronchitis infections lately."

She said she was okay, and we went on with our lunch. Toward the end she said, "I want to tell you something. I have been praying about whether to mention this to you, and the first question you asked me today was how I was feeling." She went on to say that she was a smoker and had been a smoker for many years, and the Lord had been convicting her about it. She said she wasn't ready to tell the group, which I was okay with as long as she would work with me to try and kick the habit. We came up with a plan to try and left the rest to the Lord.

As we journeyed the next few months, I would text her and ask her how she was doing with this—was she wearing her patch, chewing her gum, decreasing the amount she smoked a day, and so on. Then on one Wednesday night, unexpected to me, she confessed to the group. In my heart and mind, I was absolutely ecstatic! First, she had spoken publicly what Satan had tried to convince her to keep private. Second, she was sharing her life and letting her trusted friends and sisters in Christ in. She cried and cried as she shared this with us. The gals (of course) rallied around her and told her they loved her and she could do this! At this point, we all had the liberty to call, text, and ask her how she was doing with kicking this.

The point of all of this is that, whether it's remaining disciplined in our reading, journaling, and memorizing the Word, or whether it is confessing and choosing to see victory in our lives over sin—accountability is key! We need others in our lives who will ask us the hard questions and who will speak truth to us. Discipleship isn't always easy, but none of us would be who we are today without it. As a leader, you will have some situations that turn out wonderfully successful, and others that will wildly disappoint you, but through it all, accountability is nonnegotiable.

Everyone in the group must agree at the start to live in the light.

## Reproducible

Second Timothy 2:2 says, "What you have heard from me in the presence of many witnesses, commit to faithful men [or faithful people] who will be able to teach others also." This verse is important because it shows us the next step in what makes a healthy disciple: reproducibility.

The end goal in discipleship is always replication. If we don't replicate the process, future generations won't rise up. All throughout Scripture we are taught to remember what God has done and to tell future generations. At the beginning of journeying with a group of ladies, I always have them sign the covenant that ends with, "Begin praying about replicating the discipleship process upon completion of this group. This is not a mandate but upon completion, the hope is that I will reproduce what I have learned. Discipleship is reproducible not repeatable."

When they replicate, it doesn't have to look exactly like what I did, but my job is not done until the player becomes the coach. Still, especially early on, some ladies get a little frazzled when thinking about leading a group. When that happens, I always reassure them and tell them not to worry about it yet. We'll worry about replicating a D-Group once we establish regular spiritual disciplines that will hopefully last a lifetime. I encourage them to let the Lord do the work in their lives over the next year and we will talk about replicating closer to the end of our time together.

What I hope for, even if someone doesn't replicate exactly at the end of our time, is that at some point it hits them. I pray that if they look back and evaluate their life, they can say the time they experienced the most growth and felt the closest to the Lord was when they were in discipleship relationships.

I have seen it all too many times. Women who thrive in a D-Group for a year all of a sudden can fall off the face of the earth. They didn't replicate and didn't have any plans for their next step. I have seen their marriages fall apart, I've seen them enter into affairs, and I've seen them begin seasons of poor decision-making. Now, don't get me wrong, discipleship isn't a cure-all. It only works as long as you practice it. But when you are living in close community with others, being accountable to them, and in God's Word regularly, these bad decisions are far less likely. You will have habits to help keep you healthy.

You and I need to be in these relationships regularly—I recommend constantly. Remember discipleship is a lifestyle, not a program. It is not a light switch you turn on and off when you feel like it. Do I get tired or worn down? Sure. Do I sometimes want to stay home and miss group? Sure. But have I committed to the Lord and the ladies? Absolutely. Discipleship is a part of my day-in and day-out life regardless of how I feel. We are all always in need of these relationships and regular spiritual disciplines.

As I am sitting here typing this, I am on vacation at the beach. I'm sitting out on the balcony, watching the waves, and typing. For some reason my computer keeps going in and out of Internet service. It will pause and say "reconnecting" or "trying to connect." It's a little frustrating because my computer won't allow me to type when it's trying to reconnect. How frustrating is it to live your life in this state—constantly having to stop to re-find connection with the Creator of the Universe. The discipleship process and the disciplines of the faith keep us in that constant state of connection to the Lord. We don't have to bounce back from a lost signal and try to reconnect. Who wants to live a life of on-again, off-again? I don't know about you, but I want to live a life fully connected to my source of life where I hear from Him all around me.

One of the best ways to continue being in discipleship is to be constantly launching and starting new D-Groups. As you will find out, you always learn more when you lead. I've gotten more from leading groups than I ever would have bouncing around from leader to leader. I tell my ladies all the time, when you lead your own group you will learn way more than I can teach you. There is such joy in seeing women who have caught the passion for discipleship find the value in sharing their lives and investing into other women. One of the greatest testaments I can hear at the end of our time together is someone who says, "I can't imagine my life without discipleship!"

Still, the time to replicate is truly a bittersweet one. It's like when you drop your kids off for the first day of school. I used to cry when I would drop Rig and Ryder off at school. At the school they used to attend, they wanted to minimize everyone walking in all the time, so they encouraged us to drop them off from the car line. Against every mom-fiber in my body, I adhered and cruised through the drop-off line. As they got out of the car and started walking to the doors of the school, I put my window down and became a creeper. I crept along in the line telling them I loved them and to have a good day. As I got further and further from the doors, I was straining my neck the whole way just to make sure they made it in those doors of the school, all the while crying behind my sunglasses.

I strained my neck watching them go in for a few reasons. One, because of Rig's energy level, I never knew if he was going to actually get to class or lose focus along the way. I needed to see him cross the threshold of the school doors before I drove away. Two, I felt like half of my heart was walking away from me for the day and I was sad. This was true even at the end of the school year. I knew it was good that they were going to school, but part of my heart broke to let them go. Life is all about letting go at different ages and stages. It's similar when your D-Group replicates. It's a good thing and something that needs to happen, but part of you wants to keep straining your neck to look back. Part of you doesn't want to let go.

Letting go is good and letting go is needed. You can be sad when it ends, but before then, relish in the time you have had together. Be excited that you are about to take more ladies on that journey with you and they will feel the same way in a year's time.

At the end of our time together, which mostly always falls in December, we have an end-of-the-year Christmas party. We gather at someone's house and we bring little gifts for one another. Years ago, in our group we did a "favorite things" party, which I ended up doing every year after that: each person brings the rest of the people in the group one of their favorite things. It could be as small or as big as you want. Some ladies have given their favorite movie, lotion, lip gloss, book, pen, K-cups, hand sanitizers, and socks, just to name a few. It doesn't matter what it is; what makes it special is that it's something close to your heart. That makes it close to everyone else's too.

Treasure your time with the ladies you disciple, but be preparing along the way to encourage them to replicate what they've learned. That's the way discipleship continues, and one of the ways you know you've cultivated a healthy culture within your D-Group.

## Communal

Discipleship should not be approached with a classroom mentality; it happens in circles, not rows. It isn't a course you take or a meeting once a week. Living and journeying with a small group of women is much more than this. You become part of their daily lives. Hebrews 10:24–25 affirms this, saying, "And let us watch out for one another to provoke love and good works, not neglecting to gather together, as some are in the habit of doing, but encouraging each other, and all the more as you see the day approaching."

One of the coolest elements about a group is bringing together ladies who don't even know each other at the beginning and watching friendships form. In one of my more recent groups, only two of the ladies knew each other beforehand. I had a connection with each of them, but they didn't all know one another. I remember thinking several months into our time together that you would have thought these women had known each other for their entire lives!

No one can do relationships better than women. It is in our DNA. I don't have to promote living life with others and beg them to get together outside of our meeting times; they want to do it naturally. It's just the way we're wired.

I read a book entitled *Biblical Femininity* every year with my D-Group. It is written by Chrystie Cole, and she has really helped me to understand how women are designed by our Creator. She teaches that when God created woman in Genesis, He created a "helper fit" or a "helper suitable."

> In the original Hebrew, this is *ezer kenegdo*. *Ezer* means one who helps, one who brings that which is lacking to the aid of another. The word *kenegdo* means corresponding to. So joined together, *ezer kenegdo* means essential counterpart or corresponding strength.

She goes on to say,

. . . a woman provides an undergirding
strength within the context of relationship that empowers another to become and
achieve things that might have otherwise
been impossible. She is an essential coun-
terpart providing necessary, load-bearing
support.[16]

Now with the HGTV craze today, we all know what load-
bearing support is. When you think of a load-bearing beam
in a house that allows the support that the house needs in
order to remain standing and safe, and apply that illustra-
tion to how a woman is created, it really helps to have this
visual. The beautiful way God created a woman doesn't
only apply if she is married or not. It applies to every woman
in every stage and season of life. Whether you are a mom,
wife, daughter, sister, friend, coworker, neighbor, caretaker,
or disciple-maker, you were created to come alongside
those you are in relationship with and give strength and
support. You are able to empower them to accomplish that
which might otherwise have been impossible.

As we do this, we reflect God and bring Him glory. This
is why we can do discipleship well. Living in relationship is
truly how we have been created.

A few of the ladies in my D-Group are also in my Life
Group, which meets a few times a month. I workout with one
at the gym. One woman is my doctor and another is my chi-
ropractor, whom I see weekly. We all live life outside of the
walls of the D-Group meeting. I see the ladies together all
the time even when I am not there. Additionally, the gals in

my group do date nights together with their husbands. One friend plays tennis and some of the women have gone to her matches. Two ladies had babies that year, and now one friend has become their adopted aunt. We have all become a part of each other's lives more intimately as time has gone by.

It's so wonderful when you pray about whom the Lord will allow you to meet with over the course of a year together. These friendships and relationships will last a lifetime. These friendships have strengthened our individual faiths over this year together. We have grown in our walk with Christ through growing in life alongside one another. We have prayed together and for each other, and cried at what the Lord has done in our lives. We have rejoiced over joyous times and answered prayers, and we have watched and listened to what God has shown us all individually. There is nothing quite like the community that is formed in a D-Group. We are truly one another's load-bearing support system.

What you get in a D-Group can't be found in a Life Group, Sunday school class, Bible study class, or any large group gathering. It's more personal and intimate than that. Those other groups are good and helpful and necessary as a part of your growth, but a D-Group will take you deeper, not only in your knowledge of God, but in your living and sharing your life with others as God teaches you and works in you. You take ownership of your faith. You don't sit and listen to someone else leading and teaching in a D-Group all the time like you might in those other settings; here, you are an active participant.

Also, a D-group is always gender-exclusive, with three to six participants, whereas a Life Group, Sunday school class, or Small Group is larger in size, and usually coed. D-Groups are exclusively for believers while the others are typically inlets for believers and the lost. Another major difference is the level of accountability you receive in a D-Group that you don't receive in another setting.

The resulting community is indescribable and absolutely essential to the health of a discipleship relationship.

## Scriptural

The final mark of a healthy D-Group is also the most crucial: the Bible is always the textbook. Do not attempt to do a D-Group with a Bible study workbook. Do not pop in a DVD series. Don't turn a D-Group into a book club. If you want to do a book club or a Bible study gleaned from someone else's walk with God, you can do those groups, but don't call it discipleship. True biblical discipleship is centered around the Word of God in the life of the participants. It is the centerpiece for your group from which all other things flow. Hearing from God individually and coming together to share that and dialogue about it each week is the crux of your journey.

Don't hear what I am not saying. There are men and women out there whom God has given the wonderful gift of teaching. Praise God for them and for that gift! We need those teachers and scholars. But just because you don't have the gift of teaching doesn't mean God cannot and will not speak to you and through you; that is a lie from the enemy. I am passionate about getting women in the Word for themselves so that they can see and hear what God has for their lives. I don't want you to depend on someone else alone to relay what God has told them. God will tell *you*!

Look at all of the things the Word does for us:

> *It keeps your ways pure:* "How can a young man keep his way pure? By keeping your word. I have sought you with all my heart; don't let me wander from your commands. I have treasured your word in my heart so that I may not sin against you." (Ps. 119:9–11)

> *It blesses you and keeps you from taking counsel from the wicked:* "How happy is the one who does not walk in the advice of the wicked or stand in the pathway with sinners or sit in the company of mockers! Instead, his delight is in the LORD's instruction, and he meditates on it day and night. He is like a tree planted beside flowing streams that bears its fruit in its season and whose leaf does not wither. Whatever he does prospers. The wicked are not like this; instead, they are like chaff that the wind blows away. Therefore the wicked will not stand up in the judgment, nor sinners in the assembly of the righteous. For the LORD watches over

the way of the righteous, but the way of the wicked leads to ruin." (Ps. 1:1–6)

*It created the very universe we exist in:* "By faith we understand that the universe was created by the word of God, so that what is seen was made from things that are not visible." (Heb. 11:3)

*It teaches you how to love God with all your heart, soul, and might, and how to teach that to your children:* "Listen, Israel: The LORD our God, the LORD is one. Love the LORD your God with all your heart, with all your soul, and with all your strength. These words that I am giving you today are to be in your heart. Repeat them to your children. Talk about them when you sit in your house and when you walk along the road, when you lie down and when you get up. Bind them as a sign on your hand and let them be a symbol on your forehead. Write them on the doorposts of your house and on your city gates." (Deut. 6:4–9)

*It shows you how to be wise for salvation and equips you for every good work:* "But as for you, continue in what you have learned and firmly believed. You know those who taught

you, and you know that from infancy you
have known the sacred Scriptures, which
are able to give you wisdom for salvation
through faith in Christ Jesus. All Scripture
is inspired by God and is profitable for
teaching, for rebuking, for correcting, for
training in righteousness, so that the man
of God may be complete, equipped for every
good work." (2 Tim. 3:14–17)

*It revives your soul and gives you wisdom:*
"The instruction of the LORD is perfect,
renewing one's life; the testimony of the
LORD is trustworthy, making the inexperi-
enced wise. The precepts of the LORD are
right, making the heart glad; the command
of the LORD is radiant, making the eyes light
up. The fear of the LORD is pure, endur-
ing forever; the ordinances of the LORD are
reliable and altogether righteous. They are
more desirable than gold—than an abun-
dance of pure gold; and sweeter than honey
dripping from a honeycomb. In addition,
your servant is warned by them, and in
keeping them there is an abundant reward."
(Ps. 19:7–11)

I could keep going, but I think you see the point I am
making. Scripture should be sacred to us. As you begin
a group, find a Bible reading plan that works for you and

then stick to it. There are many options to choose from when considering a Bible reading plan. Truthfully, there are too many to list. As I said previously, my favorite way to read the Word is chronologically. It really puts the pieces together and connects the dots.

Feed yourself constantly with the Word of God and then watch as He transforms your life through it.

The MARCS (Missional, Accountable, Reproducible, Communal, and Scriptural) are how we gauge success in a discipleship group. There are things you can do to ensure that your D-Group is as effective as it can be, but they aren't necessarily metrics to gauge success. We'll discuss some of these things in the next chapter. For now, look for the MARCS in those you disciple, and you will find that life flows out of them.

# 8

# Little Adjustments That Make a Big Difference

When you look back on your childhood, you might notice that one of the most ineffective ways for your parents to get you to do something was with the reasoning "because I told you to." However, one of the easiest ways to get a positive reaction was likely with a little encouragement.

I see this play out with my own children all the time. The other day as Rig was practicing his cursive handwriting, he said, "I'm not very good at this!" and threw his pencil down in frustration. I glanced over at what he was doing and was shocked to see that his cursive handwriting looked better than his print! I exclaimed, "Rig! This looks so good!

I can't believe how neat your cursive is and how good a job you're doing!" His little face looked surprised. He looked at me with part bewilderment, part surprise, and smiled. "You can totally do this, Rig," I said, and he took off to finish. When he was done, it was even better than he expected it to be.

This is the same way most people are: they can rise to the challenge, but they need encouragement along the way.

I can't tell you how many times we hear statements like these:

> "I have a bad memory and I don't think I will be able to memorize verses."

> "I'm not really a writer and don't think my journals will be very good."

> "I don't know if I can do all of this."

As a leader, it is my responsibility to build confidence in the women I am able to meet with. I want to be the person in their corner hearing their struggles and responding with, "Oh, yes, you can!" Don't for one second think you cannot do the things I've talked about in this book. You may have a bad memory and you may struggle some with memory verses, but you and your group are going to struggle together and get through it. And you are at least going to try! Don't let fear of the unknown or fear of defeat stop you. Fear can paralyze us if we let it. And remember: God wouldn't have asked us to do this in His Word if it wasn't possible!

I was diagnosed with Hashimoto's disease last year, which is an autoimmune disease of the thyroid. There are so many symptoms that it would take me too long to list them, but one in particular is memory lapses. I have always recognized that I have a "bad" memory, but I wish I had known sooner that I could've just blamed it on Hashimoto's!

Many times I can't remember what I did a few days ago, or half the time what I ate the night before, but I can memorize and recite my verses each and every week. Sometimes people will tell me that they saw me the other day and I can't remember where they saw me. Another kicker is that I travel some and I will have friends ask me how my trip was when I get back to town and I have to stop and really think about where I just got home from! However, most of the time, I never have a problem with memory verses. Isn't that funny? You may be in the same boat, where you think you can't do this, much less lead other women in it. You might have a mountain of reasons why—your schedule is packed, you have a rough history that has done a number on your brain, or you have a disease that impairs memory function. *Despite all of that,* you can do this. You *can* memorize Scripture. You *can* read the Word daily. You *can* make disciples. And you need to encourage your ladies that they can as well.

Do not let your fear of defeat be an excuse to not try. Half our battle is a battle of the mind. My sweet mother-in-law thought for sure she would never be able to memorize verses or be in a D-Group, much less lead one, but you should see her now! She quotes her verses all the time and is leading her own group with the ease of a seasoned veteran.

Always keep in the back of your mind that you want to be encouraging and not discouraging toward your ladies. Even though you have to confront and address hard topics, issues, and sin, you never want them to feel defeated. I never want my ladies to leave disheartened because of something I said or did. Even when I had to address the habitual sexual sin I mentioned before, she knew when she left my house how much I loved her and wept for her. I told her over and over how much I desperately believed God wanted to do some amazing things in her life. I wanted her to be encouraged that there could be a different path and outcome for her.

As we talk about a few ways to enhance the experience of your D-Group for your ladies, remember a few things: never lead by intimidation, never be a know-it-all, and never convince yourself you have to have all the answers or be some supreme disciple-maker. We are all in this together! And remember Christ's example to guide you: In His omniscience, Jesus actually *was a* literal know-it-all, yet we never see Him acting like one!

## Transparency and Confidentiality

Have you noticed with the up-and-coming generations, all they want is authenticity? They want realness and truth. No more sweeping things under the rug. We aren't going to reach people unless we are willing to be transparent, open, and honest with them. As you begin leading a D-Group, make it a conscious, daily effort to be transparent and honest with the ladies you disciple. In a lot of ways, the degree to which your group works depends on how open you are with one another.

Talk about transparency before you even start your group. I go as far as to list it in the covenant we all sign at the beginning. It states that we will all contribute to an atmosphere of confidentiality, honesty, and transparency for the edification of others in the group as well as our own spiritual growth. You want to encourage this throughout your time together. Most of the time you won't have an issue with this, especially as everyone in the group warms up to each other; as your time goes on, this will become second nature. Many times, though, it is fostered when you as the leader model it for the gals in your group.

A great way to fan the flame of transparency is to share testimonies. I typically start testimony time a month or two after we have started meeting. I like to develop a little continuity before we share with one another. As soon as I feel that is happening, we start sharing our stories with one another. We share one a week for as many weeks as it takes for each woman to share. It's always our favorite time of the year. If you ask anyone who's been through a group with me, nine times out of ten, if not ten times out of ten, testimony time was the highlight of the year. It is a great way to get to know someone, let your guard down, and begin sharing your life.

*When it comes to transparency, a wise thing to consider is the level at which you share interpersonal details.* Because most of you will attend church together and will know the same people, you may want to be careful with names being shared in the group. I always encourage women that if they have something to share and need help with a certain issue that involves someone everyone knows, either don't use names or talk to the leader privately. I often talk with my ladies one-on-one. There are times they just want to talk about something privately, which is fine.

If you have to address sin in someone's life, you always do that confidentially and in private. Just like I did with the woman struggling with sexual sin, it is okay to handle this one-on-one for a season. If the woman is not experiencing victory, she may find confessing to the group to be beneficial; she will be exposing (and by doing so, crippling) sin and expanding her support system. Over time, as the ladies get more and more comfortable, they will share without needing to be prompted.

What is said and shared in the group needs to stay within the group. Many times you are dealing with private and sometimes sensitive matters that, to protect the person sharing, should be kept within the walls of your group. You shouldn't be looking to "out" anybody or spread gossip; you should be striving for personal victory over sin.

As a leader, you can use your life as an example. If you are transparent, they will be transparent. Your ladies need to know that even though you are in a leadership position, you aren't perfect and don't always have it together. Leaders shouldn't be placed on a pedestal. We have normal struggles and similar lives like every other person in the world.

A few years ago, a struggle developed in my life that threw me for a loop. It was something new that I had never experienced. It was June and we had begun to travel a lot—typical during the summer months. After a few weeks of symptoms, I started to realize I was having anxiety. That summer was a really rough one. I dealt with it privately for a few months, but it persisted and continued to be awful. Overall, I had been physically ill, lost weight, and didn't feel like myself at all. I realized I needed to go see my doctor and figure out what to do. Once we came back from the summer and our D-Group began to meet regularly again, I had a choice to make: Do I tell them what has been going on, or do I keep it to myself?

I thought back to the counsel I often gave my D-Group gals—advice like, "Don't live in isolation," "Let people into your life," "You have to be willing to do everything you ask your ladies to do," and so on. I realized that if I kept this struggle with anxiety to myself instead of sharing it with my ladies, I'd be violating all of my own instructions to them. So I decided to share my struggles.

So I did. I shared that I had been dealing with an onset of anxiety for some reason in my life. I asked them for prayer as I dealt with it, showing them that I am a real person and have real issues in my life just like everyone else. It also encouraged them to continue to be transparent.

I am always trying to figure out why God does what He does and allows what He allows. I know I will never have all the answers this side of eternity, and I know that His ways can't always be explained or understood. But I still like to see the dots connected if I can.

The summer when I was suddenly dealing with this anxiety, we had gone to Glorieta, New Mexico, for Collegiate Week. Glorieta is a special place for me because it is where Robby told me he loved me for the first time, so I was excited to accompany him while he preached to all of the college students who came to Collegiate Week. The days we were there, my anxiety was intense, and I was so discouraged.

One particular night, Robby extended an invitation. The response from the students was overwhelming. So many had come forward that there weren't enough counselors to accommodate them all. They needed anyone and everyone who was able to go to the counseling area to meet with students.

A few others and I got up and made our way to the room and were told to find a few students to meet with. I looked around and saw two girls huddled together and approached them. I asked if they had come back to talk with someone and they said yes. We sat down to talk and they proceeded to tell me what they had come forward for. I about fell over.

Have you guessed it? Yep! Anxiety.

Had I not had the roughest summer of my life, I would have had no way to relate to these girls. I shared with them about my own recent journey and we prayed together. It is just like the Lord to work in our lives and lead us to share it.

Transparency is needed and trust is necessary. We have to remember that when things can't be explained, we can simultaneously share our lament with others and also trust the God of the universe.

## Commitment

Whether you are being discipled or you are making disciples, please know you are making a commitment. You are committing first to God and then to the other group members you'll be journeying with. The covenant is crucial because it lists all the expectations and exactly what you are agreeing to—what you need to be committed to. You learn up front what will be accomplished together.

Every now and then you may have someone who slacks off in her commitment level. When this happens, it affects the whole group. You grow as a unit and you are held back as a unit. If you notice someone not following through on her commitment, you can rest assured the other ladies know it too. When this happens, if you notice that it is a pattern and not just an off-week, meet with the person one-on-one to talk about what is going on.

Like I mentioned earlier, the group accountability will work out many of these situations on their own, but I have had one instance where I had to step in and intervene.

A woman in one of my groups suddenly stopped doing some of the things the group was doing. I noticed this when we were in a period of reviewing a few weeks' worth of memory verses. We reviewed for two weeks and came together to recite them.

As we went around the table everyone knew their verses and could say them at the snap of a finger. When we got to her, she didn't know them at all. It was as if she hadn't even tried. I didn't say anything in the group because I didn't have to; it was obvious she hadn't even bothered to review them. This raised a flag in my mind because I put it together with a few other things I'd noticed over the previous few weeks. For instance, because we share our journals with each other on the app in real time, I noticed that she was not journaling. I had a feeling that if she wasn't journaling, she most likely wasn't reading her Bible either.

As soon as we left group that night, I texted her and asked to meet her for lunch that week. We only had three months left in our D-Group time together, but I didn't want her to assume she couldn't finish strong. There was no point in being in the group if it wasn't doing anything for her. Again you grow as a unit, or you are held back as a unit. If you notice something going on with one of the gals in your group, most likely everyone else recognizes it too.

We sat down and I told her why I wanted to meet with her: It seemed to me that she had given up. I asked her if she had even tried to review her verses because it didn't appear that she had. She got pretty emotional and said that no, she hadn't. She really was just struggling and having a hard time in her life, which we all knew about, but she was particularly struggling with sadness and a little depression. And that's usually the real issue going on behind a lack of consistency—a person is struggling and they just need you to enter in with them, tell them that they are seen, that you care, and that someone is there to be with them in it and help them. She cried a little bit as we talked, and I asked her if she wanted to continue on. After our talk, she told me that yes, she wanted to stay with us and that yes, she wanted to finish strong.

And she did. She totally turned it around and got back on track; we all finished together a few months after this. I loved her and wanted the best for her and had compassion for her because of some particularly difficult situations she was in, but more than ever she needed to be in the Word and to be hearing from God to get her through it. That is why I met with her and asked about what appeared to be laziness or lack of commitment. Had she not wanted to remain in the group, I would have been saddened, but I would have helped her find the next step for her at that time.

You always want to maintain the highest level of commitment in the group. If you are meeting longer than a year, another suggestion I mentioned earlier is to have the group re-sign the covenant after a year has gone by. This is a crucial step in boosting our motivation and commitment level. Trust me, when you meet longer than a year, keeping everyone motivated until the end can be challenging, but pulling out the covenant and allowing them to recommit is a helpful reminder that you should still be going strong for the next six months.

That being said, I'll remind you that the sweet spot for a D-Group is twelve months. At the end of that amount of time most of the ladies are ready to replicate. They have watched for a year and participated for a year and now they are ready to reproduce the process. It brings an element of excitement to the end of the time together.

## Leadership

In order to lead others well you have to lead yourself well, because your ladies will look to you as a model for ministering to others. This does not mean you are perfect by any means, or that you will always have it all together. Nothing could be further from the truth. You will struggle and have life issues occur during your time with your group, but they are looking to you to determine how they will handle their life, issues, and sin. Be open and honest with them along the way. Let them know you are real just like them. Part of leading is letting them into your life, struggles and all. Here are five tips I've found when it comes to being a good D-Group leader.

### 1. Don't be a know-it-all.

The beautiful thing to me about meeting with a group even though I am the leader is that they lead me too. Each week, I get to hear through their lives and their journals what God is speaking to them, and it ministers to me. It's a cyclical process; all members benefit. I need this group just as much as each of the participants do! I thrive in my pursuit of God because of these ladies alongside of me.

### 2. Be aware of pride in your life.

I had a lady call once about starting a movement of discipleship in her women's ministry at church. She was asking great questions and then mentioned one woman that gave me pause. There was a lady in her church who had been meeting with women for awhile, and once they moved on and discipled other ladies, this woman went around saying those ladies were her daughters and granddaughters in discipleship. She asked me if this was normal and if that is what we should be saying.

I said, "Uh, no." While there is some truth to what this woman was saying—yes, church members are supposed to be spiritual mothers and fathers to others—no one should feel the need to go around putting flags on people, proudly labeling them as a "discipleship granddaughter." Your investment does live on in other people as they in turn invest and make disciples, but it should not be a mark of pride in your life. *They* may talk about who discipled them, but you investing in them is not a grand spiritual accomplishment; it is you simply being obedient to what Christ called you to do. Do everything from a humble posture, and the seeds of pride can be squashed before they even sprout buds.

### 3. Never ask someone to do something you are not willing to do.

If we are memorizing verses, *I* am memorizing verses. If we are journaling, *I* am journaling. If we are reading books together, *I* am reading those books. You can't take someone on a journey you aren't willing to take.

Exceptions come up, but you work around them. For example, if I have already memorized the verse that the group is working on, I will choose another verse, but I am still memorizing. Most of the time, I read the books I assign over and over again with the group. I may have read the book four or five times, but I'll read it again to be fresh and current with the discussion. The only time I may not read the same book as the group is during the summer. I will assign a Christian biography or two for the group to read (ones that I have already read) so that I can read new material, which I am currently doing as I'm writing this book. I have read three new books so far on my vacation and I have a list of ten more! I won't get to them all, but I like to read a book most of the time before I assign it for the group so that I know what to recommend.

### 4. You lead by learning and loving your ladies.

Develop relationships with them. Pray for them. Call, text, have lunch, go for a walk, work out, go shopping, do date nights or girls night with them. These relationships are going to last longer than the time frame of your group, and they may call you for advice and counsel for years to come. Don't be detached from the group and don't lead by intimidation. The more you are a learner, the more you will lead. The more you love them, the more you lead them.

### 5. Be disciplined.

The greatest discipline of a D-Group leader is your quiet time. Your ability to manage your time and prioritize is extremely important. If you aren't doing those things, your ladies won't either. Some things in life aren't as predictable or manageable when it comes to time, but you *have* to manage this. Your quiet time won't magically happen; you have to be intentional with it. It should be a regular time on your calendar every day.

Everyone reading this book will be in different seasons of life, and will therefore have quiet times that look different from others. That's okay. Do what works for you. I'm in a season right now where I set the clock to wake up before my boys for a few reasons.

First, if I don't do my quiet time before my kids wake up, it most likely won't happen at all. Once the day's activities begin, I don't stop until my head hits the pillow. I am completely worthless at night. My brain shuts off and shuts down.

Second, I want them to see me sitting in my chair reading my Bible and spending time with the Lord every day. Every day they come down those stairs, they see me in the same place. Every day. They never come down without seeing me in my chair unless they wake up super early. I want this memory to be with them as they get older: Mom was intentional and woke up every day to spend time with Jesus. I want to model this for them. They know they can come and give me sweet morning snuggles and talk about how they slept and what they dreamed about, but they know I am not getting up from my chair until I am finished. I'll make breakfast and start the day with them once I am finished, which is normally around 6:00–6:15, but not a moment sooner. I don't want giving God their firstfriuts to be any harder than it has to be, and if my example can normalize that for them, then why would I not give them that gift?

To accomplish this, I wake up around five o'clock and they, on average, wake up an hour later. Thank heavens they sleep until 6:00 a.m. so that I have an hour for myself.

Third, I just enjoy starting my day with the Lord. I love it! I love fixing my coffee, grabbing my Bible and journal, plopping down in my chair, praying Psalm 119:18–19 over my time, sighing a big "I'm ready" sigh, and letting it all go after I have just woken up. I just let it all go from the moment I sit in my chair. I have always enjoyed starting my day like this.

I learned early on in my Christian walk that if I didn't read the Bible before I left the house in the morning, it wouldn't get done. I lead myself by prioritizing this time; I have to. When I was in college, I would read before school and before leaving the house. When I was working full-time, I would get to the office early and read at my desk.

The point is to be intentional and set aside a time that works for you to do your quiet time. You may have to go to bed early in order to do this. So what? Go to bed early! Do what you need to do in order to prioritize getting into the Word. If you can't manage your time and prioritize your quiet time, then you need to wait on leading a group until you can. Discipline is one of the primary ways you lead yourself. You have to lead yourself well in order to lead others well. Be intentional in your life in whatever way you need to.

Taking care of yourself spiritually and physically are both extremely important. The schedule that I have created allows me to do my quiet time first and then work out second. That's not how my husband operates, though. He works out first thing when he wakes up, showers and gets ready, and then sits down to do his quiet time before he leaves for the day. Regardless of the particular order in which we do things, the point is that we are both intentional with our time, setting our clocks to wake up, knowing what we want to accomplish before we leave for the day.

In order to be intentional with our mornings we have to be intentional with our nights. It means I don't stay up all hours of the night. I can't function well like that. It's a recipe for disaster. I don't like to be tired and dragging the next day either. Robby nicknamed me "Snapper" years ago, which stands for snapping turtle. He will not hesitate to tell me that I have woken up on the wrong side of the shell if I am in a bad mood for some reason. Though this doesn't happen often, if I don't get enough sleep, it does. I am an eight-hour-a-night sleeper. It is what I really need to be at my best, so I try to plan to get in the bed in order to get that amount of sleep. I mean, who wants to be a snapper, right?

Now, when the summer rolls around, I let myself stay up later than usual because I know I can wake up later and still have my same schedule. I don't have to rush out the door to be anywhere most summer mornings. I do the same thing on Christmas break. (I like having that time to stay up late and watch Hallmark movies! Anybody else with me?)

The point is not to be so legalistic that there's no room for flexibility. Your day won't always look the same and there will be times when you may plan things a certain way but it just doesn't happen the way you intended. That is fine.

Don't beat yourself up because you have become so dogmatic about your schedule. Above all, be intentional with your time and prioritize your spiritual and physical health. The point is to manage your time or your time will manage you. Are you getting tired of me saying that yet?

Many of you reading this may work full-time. If you find it hard to wake up earlier than you already do, try listening to your Bible in audio form while you put on your makeup. There was a time when I did this regularly. The boys were younger and it didn't matter what time I tried to wake up, there was no set schedule. One thing I could guarantee is that there would be crying, feeding, and changing diapers going on! I would listen to my Bible and often voice record a journal in the car. A staff wife and mom who was a little bit older and wiser once encouraged some of us younger moms to just open our Bible and leave it on the table. This way when we would sit down for lunch or sit down to feed the kiddos we could read a little bit.

If you're a student, you could plan to meet with God between classes at a campus coffee shop. If you work the late shift in your job, you could prioritize meeting with the Lord an hour or so before you go in. If you minister to students, choose a time to read the Word on campus, between common class times when the students are unavailable to meet with you. If you're a barista who has to be at work by 5:00 a.m. to have the coffee ready by 6:00 a.m., perhaps waking up early isn't attainable; that's okay, make a plan to meet with God before you head to bed and process the day with Him. If you're retired, perhaps you could choose a time right before a certain task you do daily—just before lunchtime or right before your daily walk. If you travel a lot for work or personal reasons, listen to the Bible during commutes or layovers. Just make sure whatever time slot you choose actually works for you and that you stick with it on a daily basis.

However it looks for you, I cannot reiterate this last point enough: Manage your time. Discipleship is not something that happens by accident, and it is not something that you can coast through. Let your ladies speak to you and invest in you too. Beware of pride. Prioritize your quiet time. Lead yourself so that you can lead others. And as you do all of this, do it with the joy of chasing after your Father. You'll find that the resulting D-Groups will be among the most fulfilling relationships you've ever had.

9

# The Devastating Effects of Not Making Disciples

There are two things that my life would be noticeably worse without (apart from the Lord, of course): my family and coffee. Okay, maybe there are a few others too. I also love hot, hot showers.

And sea salt caramel chocolate. And the beach. I felt better about this last one after I read Charles Spurgeon's biography by Arnold Dalimore a few years ago, because he noted that Spurgeon would get sick during the year and he would go to a certain place near the seaside and spend time there recuperating. I feel like that when I'm at the beach. I sit there in awe of God and His creation and I feed my soul with rest, reading, and writing. I get to watch my kids swim and play games and enjoy uninterrupted time together . . . it is heaven on earth for me.

It's funny, but thinking about doing without certain things in my life always brings me back to discipleship. I cannot imagine this command of God not being in my life. I thirst for it and desire it above anything else I find myself doing. It keeps me inspired, motivated, growing, and living life with others instead of in isolation. It feeds my soul and keeps me accountable. I could read my Bible and memorize Scripture on my own, but at some point I would run out of steam. My life would get "too busy" or I would just let things fall by the wayside. But having a group of ladies in my life to whom I am accountable reduces my chance of falling off the wagon to near zero. It is such a part of me that I honestly cannot imagine my life without it.

If you are doing life without discipleship, you are missing out on one of the most fulfilling things you can experience. First, you're missing rich fellowship and accountability. We need other people because the journey, though it is joyous, is also arduous. We need those close women to spur us on when life demands it.

Proverbs 27:17 tells us, "Iron sharpens iron, and one person sharpens another." Believe this: You don't have to go through life alone, having no women running toward Jesus alongside you. Christ journeyed with His disciples constantly. His inner three (Peter, James, and John) were with Him more often than the others were. They experienced intimate, miraculous, and challenging times as they lived life together. Perhaps Jesus needed those men just as much as they needed Him—He was fully God, but He was also fully human, desiring close, personal connections with others. The kinds of connections you make in a D-Group are the ones that will last a lifetime. As many will often say, even Jesus was in a D-Group!

Without women to walk with, you also miss out on realizing what your true wealth is in Christ and what the beauty of a walk with Him is. If you aren't learning, reading, and knowing God on a deeper level as you go through life, you are missing a piece of who you are, a connection with your Creator. How will you know who you are in Christ? How will you understand the richness of Scripture unless you are in the Word and hearing from God yourself? How will you make mature and godly decisions without seeking the Word and godly counsel? We have everything in God, and our walk with Him is unique and very specific and purposeful. I don't want to miss a thing!

The women I disciple help me to see that in my life, and I help them to see it in theirs. We remind each other of what God has said and what the Scriptures say. We challenge each other when we need it. We comfort each other in sad and difficult times. Even the most reclusive of people are built with a deep soul-longing for exactly the type of community a D-Group provides.

Perhaps most important, though, if you neglect discipleship, you ignore the only strategy given by God to the church to reach the world. God's "Plan A" for the church has always been: "Go, therefore, and make disciples of all nations, baptizing them in the name of the Father and of the

Son and of the Holy Spirit, teaching them to observe everything I have commanded you" (Matt. 28:19–20a).

But notice this too: His plan has a built-in comfort. The end of Matthew does not stop at where I cut it off; it continues, "And remember, I am with you always, to the end of the age" (Matt. 28:20b). It makes my heart happy to dwell on that! Jesus assured us that He is with us not just some days and during some times, but to *the end of the age*. You cannot be more present with someone than that. In every situation, in all things good and bad, happy or sad, He is with me!

God's strategy was to be with us and in us in order to replicate what He had done on this earth with others. That is His plan for His people. No one else made this up. I don't know about you, but I want to be involved and included in the promise He gave to His people. I want to be growing and not sitting on the sidelines. I want to be active in my faith and not just storing up a bunch of knowledge for myself.

Obedience is something we teach our boys constantly. You may be in the same boat right now. Raising young children is tough work! Something we say to our children is that we want immediate obedience. Not delayed obedience. Not half-way obedience. No parent wants their child to disobey them. The problem with many of us, though, is we delay our obedience or just downright disobey our Father when it comes to the command to make disciples. Let us not neglect the Great Commission. We need to be children who practice immediate obedience. Wouldn't you agree that obedience is so rewarding? When I obey commands from the Lord in my life there is peace, contentment, and happiness.

There is no greater joy for me than when women tell me they have never memorized more Scripture and have never been in the Bible more consistently in their lives. I hear it every year and my heart does cartwheels because I know they can't imagine their life without these disciplines as well. They have caught the passion and the mission and that is all I can ask for.

But just because this is God's plan for the Church—and for you, specifically—doesn't mean it won't come without hurdles. We're imperfect people, after all, and so there will be certain times in your D-Group where you experience frustration.

## Frustrations within a D-Group

I won't lie or act like there aren't times I feel frustration bubbling over inside of me. Sometimes women slack on their reading, fall behind without remorse on journaling, don't make it a priority to show up, and close themselves off from being transparent. When you experience any one of these from a D-Group participant it can be extremely frustrating.

I try to discuss these issues on the front end of a group by listing them in the covenant, but still there will be negative patterns that develop and need to be addressed. When addressing these things, I always err on the side of grace. In the event I have to mention attendance to someone, I try to find out if everything is okay in her life, and mention to her that we have missed her. I don't go in and attack someone because they have missed a few weeks. My primary goal is not to offend or wound her, but draw her back in and remind her of our commitment.

If someone does not want to join in the discussion or open up and be transparent, it affects the atmosphere of the whole room. One time I had to talk to a girl who was present in the group but not really "present" in our midst. The longer it went unaddressed, the more bothersome it became. So I pulled her aside one night and discussed it with her. She mentioned that she was just overwhelmed and was afraid of saying something wrong—an issue I cleared up immediately. I reassured her that we were not there to attack or belittle her, but that we were all in this together. After that, she did better with adding to our conversation. It's your job as a leader to make sure you head off any troubles before they can grow into thorns. You have to have dialogue among the group members for it to thrive.

If you encounter someone who has trouble opening up, it may help to draw them in with icebreaker questions. It may help to change the location you meet to somewhere she feels more comfortable. Sometimes a different setting can change the mood and feel.

Someone not doing her daily reading, journaling, or memorization of weekly verses can cause frustration not only for the leader but for the group members—if everyone is putting in the work but one, there can be natural resentment that grows. This, too, is an excellent moment for you to pull that member aside and gently ask how she's doing—what she's struggling with, what she needs from you, and what you can work together on to make her experience better.

Sometimes you may not even notice it, but a woman will come to you frustrated with herself because she is struggling in an area and needs some help figuring it all out. Once I had a group member who had gotten behind on journaling and I hadn't really noticed. She came to me and said she was behind and not really sure what to do. I told her to jump back in and start again. I told her not to worry about catching up but just start from where she was now. If she needed to journal once a week for a while that was fine, but I asked her to work up to two times a week. Once she felt the burden lift, she was able to get back on track.

Often I have found that the ladies know when they have slacked off or when they've had an off week. I don't have to say it or bring it up. Sitting around the room and going over all we have done together speaks for itself. Someone will say, "I don't have my verse tonight but I will have it next week." There you go! I didn't say a word. The group functioning as it should did it for me. As you keep your group healthy, you will find that many situations work themselves out so long as you are remaining focused on the goal at hand: becoming more like Christ today than you were yesterday.

# 10

# Leaving a Lasting Legacy

After all we've explored in this book, you may be asking, "Now what?"

My prayer for you is that you would see the value of discipleship in your own life and desire to follow the call to make disciples. Often, someone doesn't know how to start or what to do, so they do nothing at all. That is the reason for this book. I wanted to create something that would not only encourage you to make disciples, but would be a road map to success. I envision this being a reference book that can be picked up over and over again for guidance or reminders of what we need to be doing.

Remember, discipleship is *reproducible*, not repeatable. There's a difference. Your process doesn't have to look exactly like what I have laid out and described in this book. That would be a *repeat* or carbon copy of all the ways *I* disciple. Hopefully, you have gained some insight and ideas to get started, and have found some tips that you can implement in your own endeavors. With those tools in hand, you can make your discipleship process your own—complete with your own creative ideas and your own personality woven in. That's what *reproducing* discipleship is.

Though you certainly have the flexibility to make your D-Group your own, if you get one thing from all that I have said, please get this: the Bible must be the essential element to your disciple-making process. Choose a reading plan, a method, or assign regular Bible reading to incorporate into your group and center everything else on that.

R. C. Sproul said, "Burning hearts are not nourished by empty heads." In order to burn with passion for Christ we must feed our minds with the Word. We must spend time in the Word so we can live the Word. When we spend time in the Word we are spending time with Jesus. Do you remember how Jesus explained the Scriptures to the disciples on the Emmaus road in Luke 24? Do you remember what they said in response? Verse 32 tells us: "They said to each other, 'Weren't our hearts burning within us while he was talking with us on the road and explaining the Scriptures to us?'" Time around the Scriptures creates the burning-hot heart we all want for God.

Belief drives behavior. It is important to remember that. What we believe in will affect the way we live and make decisions. What goes into our mind shapes our beliefs, which in turn guides our hearts. Jen Wilkin says, "The heart cannot love what the mind does not know. Right thinking will beget right feeling."[17]

Teach your ladies that God can, will, and does speak to them if they seek Him and spend time with Him. Record what He says. As I've said before, one thing I get excited about is the fact that my boys will have my journals one day. They will see the prayers I prayed for them as well as prayers for myself, my husband, and our ministry. God has spoken to me in countless ways, and it is recorded for them to see.

I have been learning lots about livestock lately. Not necessarily because I wanted to but because my city-boy-pastor husband has decided to become a farmer on the side. We purchased six acres a few years ago not too far from our church. Robby decided he wanted to fence in part of it and get a goat. I told him he could get whatever he wanted as long as I don't have to take care of it. I want no other responsibility than what I already have, which is two boys and three canine girls.

Well, he took that and ran with it. Our one goat turned into a few goats. Then it was a few sheep. Then, of course, a mini donkey is required to keep the coyotes away. You are beginning to hear the sarcasm in my tone, right? What's hilarious is that we knew nothing about taking care of these animals. We already had two goldendoodles, Annie Roux and Nola Rouge (we are originally from Louisiana), and a little teddy bear puppy, Ruby Rose, who are basically children to us. When the man came to drop off all of our crew, he said to Robby, "Oh yeah, the donkey is pregnant."

Robby froze, not knowing how he was going to tell me that not only would we have seven animals on our farm, but one of them was having a baby. Are you kidding?

Overall, I took the news pretty good. I stuck to my guns though. I was not taking care of anything. The man said you can sell the baby once it's born, but I told Robby we can't do that! No way, I said. We are not going to separate the momma and the baby. So now we—and by we, I mean Robby—currently have eleven animals.

At the end of the day, I just wanted Robby to have an outlet that helps him unwind. Fishing and farming are what he enjoys. He loves to go out every single day and feed the animals "special" food so they will come to him and he can pet them. It's really awesome because the boys go with him and it gets them out of the house.

I know you want to know all of their names, so let me tell you. Daisy is the pregnant mini donkey and she is a beautiful little donkey. We have one regular-size goat named Munchie and she rules the roost. We have three dwarf goats named Brownie, Blackie, and Ellie (I named her after Jim Elliott!). Then we have two sheep named Lottie and Lucy. You guessed it. Lottie is named after Lottie Moon, the missionary. These animals are quite entertaining!

Here is the thing, though. In all seriousness, I am learning a lot about the Lord through watching the sheep. I have noticed that the two sheep, Lottie and Lucy, stick together everywhere they go and they always follow Munchie, the goat. If Munchie takes off across the field, Lottie and Lucy follow. If Munchie lays in the feeding trough at night (which she often does), Lottie and Lucy are sitting on the ground right beneath her. They trail behind Munchie everywhere she goes. Do you know what that shows me? It shows me that sheep are going to follow someone or something. The question is: Who will they follow?

Jesus says in John 10:27–30:

> "My sheep hear my voice, I know them, and they follow me. I give them eternal life, and they will never perish. No one will snatch them out of my hand. My Father, who has given them to me, is greater than all. No one is able to snatch them out of the Father's hand. I and the Father are one."

We are all created to follow someone. It is in our design. The question is: Whom will you follow? The world or Jesus? The world disciples people all day long. It is time for Christians to rise up and invest in the undiscipled, or wrongly discipled, believers in our churches today. Teach them above all else to love God and love people. Teach them to invite and invest. Teach them to share not only the gospel but their very lives (1 Thess. 2:8).

Tragedy struck on our farm a year ago. It truly taught me so much. I was actually sitting in my chair working on my computer at the time. Robby and Ryder were in the living room watching a football game. Rig was sleeping next to me because he had been sick and was exhausted. Robby just happened to pause the game to check his phone when I heard what I thought was Daisy hollering. I sat for a moment and then I could faintly hear a dog and what sounded like a child screaming. I jumped up and went to the window and looked out. A dog had gotten into our fence and was running around like crazy chasing the animals. I yelled to Robby to hurry and go down to the animals because a dog was in the fence. It was freezing outside so he rushed to get his coat, gloves, and hat on, and Ryder did the same. They started up the ATV and, in the meantime, I was on the front porch clapping as loud as I could to try and distract this dog who was running rampant and barking.

The owner of the dog lives on the adjancent property, and I could hear her calling the dog's name and trying to get her to come back home. While I was on the porch trying to distract the dog, she managed to get Lottie away from the rest of the pack. Lottie was scared as could be and running to flee. I saw her fall down and the dog was biting at her ankles as she kept trying to get up but couldn't. Robby and Ryder raced down and cut a donut right by the dog to chase it off. The dog ran to the opposite side of the field and started to chase the other animals. At this point, the owner of the dog had gotten into our fence and was screaming for her dog to stop and come to her. Robby was screaming and had his BB gun ready to go if the dog tried to attack another one of our animals.

At this point, I had run halfway toward the action, thinking I was going to have to jump the fence to try and save the other animals. I had no jacket or shoes on, but I didn't know what else to do. Finally, the owner was able to grab her dog. After the commotion settled, we looked back and Lottie was still on the ground, not moving. I saw

Robby pick her up and bring her to the small shelter we had built for them. He came to the house and said he needed to go back down and see if she was okay. He said she wasn't moving much but she may have been worn out or in shock. He called a few other guys to ask their thoughts and then headed back down.

He came back shortly with one of our trusted friends who lives around the corner. They proceeded to tell me that they were going to have to put Lottie down because she broke her neck. She had run into the fence when she was trying to escape the dog and that's how we thought she broke her neck. We were all heartbroken. It was such a sad situation. The men went and put her down and our friend buried her for us. Ryder cried and cried. He crawled up in my lap and just cried. Rig woke up to him crying, and then he cried. We all had become attached to our animals and the thought of one being gone was very emotional for us, especially the boys.

As I sat there and began processing what had just happened, the Lord showed me quite a few things that I want to share.

First, I couldn't understand why Daisy didn't chase the dog and buck her away. Then it hit me. While I was watching from the window, I saw the dog manage to get Lottie by herself. Instead of staying with the rest of the herd, she took off running on her own. She left the protection of the group. Daisy had stayed with the group and didn't follow after Lottie. The bottom line is that the dog found a way to isolate Lottie. She was alone.

Here is the deal. The enemy wants nothing more than to get us off on our own and by ourselves so he can destroy our lives! The devil seeks to steal, kill, and destroy (John 10:10), and he's always looking for opportunities to isolate us, and then strike. Had Lottie stayed with the group, she would have had more protection. The same goes for us.

Discpleship affords us the kind of protection that a herd does. It's a pack, a close-knit group surrounding you and helping to guard you from wandering off by yourself. Just as Daisy alerted us to the situation, the ladies in your life will be able to sense when something is off in your life, and alert you. They will be able to help warn you of very real danger you are in, though you probably won't sense it yourself.

Second, what a visual Robby gave me as he raced down there to save his sheep! A picture of the Father at all costs rushing in to save His own. I mean, that is something! When Robby arrived, that dog took off running in the opposite direction. Satan flees when God is present! The enemy cannot and will not ever have victory over our Almighty God!

Now, the dog didn't stop right away. She decided she would just go to the opposite side of the yard and try to chase the other animals until Robby came over again and chased her off. Satan may try repeatedly to tempt us and tear us away from Christ and our community. We must stay strong in the Word and in our discipling relationships so we are ready and as protected as is humanly possible.

Third, the sheep story led me to imagine what it was like every time the Israelites celebrated Passover. They would have to go out and kill a lamb that the family had. To atone for their sin, blood had to be shed from an unblemished lamb. The lamb may have been around the family for years, raised for this purpose. How sad. Thank heavens God had provided a way to atone for their sin, but how sad that it required the death of an animal.

Even more sorrowful is that it would take the life of Christ to be our ultimate once-and-for-all sacrifice. It is sad, tragic, and triumphant all in one. We experienced what it was like to feel the loss of a lamb we loved. It was a great reminder of how much we love Christ and the sacrifice He made for us on the cross. And also it was a great reminder that death is not final for us as believers. We have hope!

Every night as I put the boys to bed, I say a prayer over them and sing a song. Every single night this is our routine. Even if I am out of town, they will call me for their prayers and song. The song I sing is always the same. When I was little my dad always sang "You Are My Sunshine" to me, so that is what I sing to my boys too. If you know that song, the second verse is a sad one, so I have changed the words to be happy instead. Ryder will not go to sleep until I sing this to him. Often, he will fall asleep even as I am singing.

My boys, like many kids I'm sure, don't like to go to bed at night. They want to be with Mom and Dad. They will tell me how they are just so sad because they won't see me until the morning and they will miss me. I tell them I will miss them too, but I am just downstairs. I am not far away and I'll see them in the morning.

I always pray for them to have a sweet and peaceful night's sleep. We pray for no bad dreams, only dreams of angels and heavenly things. I pray the Aaronic blessing over them which is in Numbers 6:24–26. It says, "May the LORD bless you and protect you; may the LORD make his face shine on you and be gracious to you; may the LORD look with favor on you and give you peace." I pray that they wake up refreshed and ready for the next day. Then I end with singing "You Are My Sunshine." It is something about those last words I say to them that are so comforting to them before I walk out of their bedroom. It lets them know they can rest peacefully until I see them in the morning.

Just like I leave my boys each night with my last words—a prayer and a song—Jesus left the disciples with some departing words too. And just like my words are comforting to my boys, the Lord's words were comforting to His followers and should be to us today.

Do you remember the last words Jesus said to His disciples in the book of Matthew? He gave them a command. In my opinion, the very last thing He said is quite comforting, or it should be, to us.

> Jesus came near and said to them, "All authority has been given to me in heaven and on earth. Go, therefore, and make disciples of all nations, baptizing them in the name of the Father and of the Son and of

the Holy Spirit, teaching them to observe everything I have commanded you. And remember, I am with you always, even to the end of the age." (Matt. 28:18–20)

If that wasn't enough, Luke records what Jesus says before His ascension in Acts 1:8, "But you will receive power when the Holy Spirit has come on you, and you will be my witnesses in Jerusalem, in all Judea and Samaria, and to the end of the earth." The disciples would not only have Jesus' presence through the indwelling of the Holy Spirit, but they would also receive power. His presence and power should give us the peace to obey Him in His commands to us.

He is never far away and will be with us always and forever!

So knowing that, what are you waiting for? Go, disciple her!

Use the Word of God, the work of God in your own life, and the wonder of God's Spirit and empowerment to invest in women. I pray the Lord blesses you and keeps you. I pray the Lord makes His face to shine upon you and is gracious to you in your efforts and endeavors to make disciples. May the Lord look with favor on you and give you peace. My hope and desire is that this has equipped you to start on your journey, and that you will be able to reference the content in this book for years to come.

Love and blessings to you as you go disciple her!

# APPENDIX 1

# Suggested Reading List

*Bearing Fruit,* Robby Gallaty

*Biblical Femininity,* Chrystie Cole

*Bonhoeffer,* Eric Metaxes

*Charles Spurgeon,* Arnold Dalimore

*Choose Wisely, Live Fully,* Donna Gaines

*Counterfeit Gods,* Tim Keller

*Firmly Planted,* Robby Gallaty

*Freefall to Fly,* Rebekah Lyons

*Growing Up,* Robby Gallaty

*Hiding in the Light,* Rifqa Bary

*The Hiding Place,* Corrie Ten Boom

*Hope Heals,* Katherine & Jay Wolf

*Hudson Taylor's Spritual Secret,* Dr. and Mrs. Howard Taylor

*I Will Carry You,* Angie Smith

*If You Only Knew,* Jamie Ivey

*My Heart,* Julie Manning

*Parenting: 14 Gospel Principles That Can Radically Change Your Family,* Paul David Tripp

*Rediscovering Disicpleship,* Robby Gallaty

*The Lost Art of Disciplemaking,* Leroy Eims

*The Master Plan of Evangelism* by Robert E. Coleman

*The Master Plan of Discipleship* by Robert E. Coleman

*This Momentary Marriage,* John Piper

*Through Gates of Splendor,* Elisabeth Elliot

*What Is the Gospel?,* Greg Gilbert

*Why Trust the Bible?,* Greg Gilbert

*Women of the Word,* Jen Wilkin

# APPENDIX 2

# Covenant Examples

## Discipleship Covenant

*"If you continue in my word, you really are my disciples. You will know the truth, and the truth will set you free." (John 8:31–32)*

Discipleship is a vital part of growth in the life of a believer and follower of Jesus Christ. Typically, if a person does not make a commitment to follow through and is not held accountable, they will start the process of discipleship strong but will not finish strong. Please pray and ask God to reveal if your schedule permits for you to be part of this D-Group. If you are married, please speak with your husband and pray with your husband about the expectations before making a commitment. I can assure you, if you are willing to make the next twelve months a priority in your life, it will be life-changing!

*I will commit to the following expectations:*

- Attend weekly meetings, unless providentially hindered. Each week we will meet for one and a half hours, and we will go through the Foundations (F-260) Bible reading plan over the next twelve months. I urge you again to make this a priority and if at any time it appears that this is not a priority, I may have to ask you to resign from the group. This is in no way meant to be discouraging, but rather to ensure each group member holds a strong commitment to the study of God's Word and to hold one another accountable. Accountability is essential for an effective D-Group.

- Memorize the assigned Scripture(s) and recite each week, read the daily assigned Scripture passages, and journal at least two times during the week about what God is revealing to you.

- Contribute to an atmosphere of confidentiality, honesty, and transparency for the edification of others in the group, as well as for your own spiritual growth.

- Make every effort to read the additional books assigned in the course of the twelve months. Books assigned will help to equip you in developing as a leader for your own group as well as aiding in your own personal spiritual growth. (No more than four or five books will be assigned.)

- Pray every week for the other women who are on this journey with you.
- Attend weekly corporate worship and regularly be involved with a life group in addition to this D-Group. (This is the pathway that our church feels is the most effective for growth in the life of a believer.)
- Begin praying about replicating the discipleship process upon completion of this group. This is not a mandate, but upon completion, the hope is that you will reproduce what you have learned. This comes in many forms. Discipleship is reproducible not repeatable.

I have prayed about being a part of this D-Group, and I commit to making every effort to fulfill the expectations listed above.

Your Signature_____

## Disciple-Making Covenant

I will commit to the following expectations:

1. I pledge myself fully to the Lord with the anticipation that I am entering a time of accelerated spiritual transformation.
2. I will meet with my D-Group for approximately one and one-half hours every week, unless providentially hindered.
3. I will complete all assignments on a weekly basis before my D-Group meeting in order to contribute to the discussion.
4. I will contribute to an atmosphere of confidentiality, honesty, and transparency for the edification of others in the group as well as for my own spiritual growth.
5. I will pray every week for the other men/women who are on the discipleship journey with me.
6. I will begin praying about replicating the discipleship process upon completion of this group.

Signed _____

Date _____

Mentee _____

Mentor _____

# APPENDIX 3

# Sample H.E.A.R. Entry

## H (Highlight)

Highlight the passage I'll be studying today: "I am able to do all things through him who strengthens me." (Phil. 4:13)

## E (Explain)

Paul was telling the church at Philippi that he had discovered the secret of contentment. No matter the situation in Paul's life, he realized that Christ was all he needed, and Christ was the one who strengthened him to persevere through difficult times.

## A (Apply)

Apply generally: In my life, I will experience many ups and downs. My contentment is not found in circumstances; rather, it is based on my relationship with Jesus Christ.

Only Jesus gives me the strength I need to be content in every circumstance of life.

Apply specifically: Right now, I feel discontent in my current work situation. I wish God would provide me with a higher income, and I often think that more money would make me more content. However, the truth is that God is where I should find my contentment, regardless of how much money my job produces. This week, I will spend my QT in passages that help realign my focus toward God and away from money, leaving my money worries at the cross, trusting that God will provide all I need.

## R (Respond)

Lord Jesus, please help me as I strive to be content in You. In Your strength, I can make it through any situation I must face.

# APPENDIX 4

# Your Process at a Glance

Below is a worksheet you can fill out or use as a checklist to help you as you plan your own process to make disciples.

**Prayer** (List the names of the ladies you are praying about asking to journey with you.)

_____

_____

_____

_____

_____

_____

## Plan Your Process

Time frame: _____
(twelve or eighteen months)
Bible Reading Plan: _____
(choose one)
Journals per week: _____
(How many journals will you expect?)

## Prepare

Covenant: _____
(Did you draft a covenant?)
Info Sheet: _____
(Will you include an info sheet?)
Invitation: _____
(Have you contacted each lady?)
Spiritual Assessment: _____
(Will you use a spiritual assessment?)

## Proceed

Meeting day and time: _____
(What day and time did you decide on?)

# APPENDIX 5

# Sample Info Sheet

*(You can add or take away questions
and make this your own.)*

Name:

Husband's name:

Children's names and ages:

Favorite color:

Favorite place to eat:

Favorite type of food:

Favorite candy bar:

Favorite place to shop:

Hobbies:

Spiritual Gift(s):

Favorite Bible verse or character and why:

Place to which you would like to travel and why:

Favorite author/book:

What are you looking forward to most by participating in a D-Group?

Who is your role model and why?

Do you have any goals you want to accomplish in life?

# F260 BIBLE READING PLAN

## A BIBLE READING PLAN FOR BUSY BELIEVERS

**WEEK 1**
Genesis 1 -2
Genesis 3-4
Genesis 6-7
Genesis 8-9
Job 1-2

Memory Verses:
Genesis 1:27
Hebrews 11:7

**WEEK 2**
Job 38-39
Job 40-42
Genesis 11-12
Genesis 15
Genesis 16-17

Memory Verses:
Hebrews 11:6
Hebrews 11:8-10

**WEEK 3**
Genesis 18-19
Genesis 20-21
Genesis 22
Genesis 24
Genesis 25:19-34, 26

Memory Verses:
Romans 4:20-22
Hebrews 11:17-19

**WEEK 4**
Genesis 27-28
Genesis 29-30:24
Genesis 31-32
Genesis 33, 35
Genesis 37

Memory Verses:
2 Corinthians 10:12
1 John 3:18

**WEEK 5**
Genesis 39-40
Genesis 41
Genesis 42-43
Genesis 44-45
Genesis 46-47

Memory Verses:
Romans 8:28-30
Ephesians 3:20-21

**WEEK 6**
Genesis 48-49
Genesis 50 – Exodus 1
Exodus 2-3
Exodus 4-5
Exodus 6-7

Memory Verses:
Genesis 50:20
Hebrews 11:24-26

**WEEK 7**
Exodus 8-9
Exodus 10-11
Exodus 12
Exodus 13:17-14
Exodus 16-17

Memory Verses:
John 1:29
Hebrews 9:22

**WEEK 8**
Exodus 19-20
Exodus 24-25
Exodus 26-27
Exodus 28-29
Exodus 30-31

Memory Verses:
Exodus 20:1-3
Galatians 5:14

**WEEK 9**
Exodus 32-33
Exodus 34-36:1
Exodus 40
Leviticus 8-9
Leviticus 16-17

Memory Verses:
Exodus 33:16
Matthew 22:37-39

**WEEK 10**
Leviticus 23
Leviticus 26
Numbers 11-12
Numbers 13-14
Numbers 16-17

Memory Verses:
Leviticus 26:13
Deuteronomy 31:7-8

**WEEK 11**
Numbers 20, 27:12-23
Numbers 34-35
Deuteronomy 1-2
Deuteronomy 3-4
Deuteronomy 6-7

Memory Verses:
Deuteronomy 4:7
Deuteronomy 6:4-9

**WEEK 12**
Deuteronomy 8-9
Deuteronomy 30-31
Deuteronomy 32:48-52, 34
Joshua 1-2
Joshua 3-4

Memory Verses:
Joshua 1:8-9
Psalm 1:1-2

Ezra 5-6

Memory Verses:
Daniel 6:26-27
Daniel 9:19

## WEEK 27
Zechariah 1:1-6, 2, 12
Ezra 7-8
Ezra 9-10
Esther 1-2
Esther 3-4

Memory Verses:
Zephaniah 3:17
1 Peter 3:15

## WEEK 28
Esther 5-7
Esther 8-10
Nehemiah 1-2
Nehemiah 3-4
Nehemiah 5-6

Memory Verses:
Deuteronomy 29:29
Psalm 101:3-4

## WEEK 29
Nehemiah 7-8
Nehemiah 9
Nehemiah 10
Nehemiah 11
Nehemiah 12

Memory Verses:
Nehemiah 6:9
Nehemiah 9:6

## WEEK 30
Nehemiah 13
Malachi 1
Malachi 2
Malachi 3
Malachi 4

Memory Verses:
Psalm 51:17
Colossians 1:19-20

## WEEK 31
Luke 1
Luke 2
Matthew 1-2
Mark 1
John 1

Memory Verses:
John 1:1-2
John 1:14

## WEEK 32
Matthew 3-4
Matthew 5
Matthew 6
Matthew 7
Matthew 8

Memory Verses:
Matthew 5:16
Matthew 6:33

## WEEK 33
Luke 9:10-62
Mark 9-10
Luke 12
John 3-4
Luke 14

Memory Verses:
Luke 14:26-27
Luke 14:33

## WEEK 34
John 6
Matthew 19:16-30
Luke 15-16
Luke 17:11-37, 18
Mark 10

Memory Verses:
Mark 10:45
John 6:37

## WEEK 35
John 11, Matthew 21:1-13
John 13
John 14-15
John 16
Matthew 24:1-31

Memory Verse:
John 13:34-35
John 15:4-5

## WEEK 36
Matthew 24:32-51
John 17
Matthew 26:35-27:31
Matthew 27:32-66,
Luke 23:26-56
John 19

Memory Verses:
Luke 23:34
John 17:3

## WEEK 37
Mark 16
Luke 24
John 20-21
Matthew 28
Acts 1

Memory Verses:
Matthew 28:18-20
Acts 1:8

## WEEK 38
Acts 2-3
Acts 4-5
Acts 6
Acts 7
Acts 8-9

Memory Verse:
Acts 2:42
Acts 4:31

## WEEK 39
Acts 10-11
Acts 12
Acts 13-14
James 1-2
James 3-5

Memory Verses:
James 1:2-4
James 2:17

**WEEK 40**
Acts 15-16
Galatians 1-3
Galatians 4-6
Acts 17-18:17
1 Thessalonians 1-2

Memory Verses:
Acts 17:11
Acts 17:24-25

**WEEK 41**
1 Thessalonians 3-5
2 Thessalonians 1-3
Acts 18:18-28, 19
1 Corinthians 1-2
1 Corinthians 3-4

Memory Verses:
1 Corinthians 1:18
1 Thessalonians 5:23-24

**WEEK 42**
1 Corinthians 5-6
1 Corinthians 7-8
1 Corinthians 9-10
1 Corinthians 11-12
1 Corinthians 13-14

Memory Verses:
1 Corinthians 10:13
1 Corinthians 13:13

**WEEK 43**
1 Corinthians 15-16
2 Corinthians 1-2
2 Corinthians 3-4
2 Corinthians 5-6
2 Corinthians 7-8

Memory Verses:
Romans 1:16-17
1 Corinthians 15:3-4

**WEEK 44**
2 Corinthians 9-10
2 Corinthians 11-13

Romans 1-2, Acts 20:1-3
Romans 3-4
Romans 5-6

Memory Verses:
Romans 5:1
2 Corinthians 10:4

**WEEK 45**
Romans 7-8
Romans 9-10
Romans 11-12
Romans 13-14
Romans 15-16

Memory Verses:
Romans 8:1
Romans 12:1-2

**WEEK 46**
Acts 20-21
Acts 22-23
Acts 24-25
Acts 26-27
Acts 28

Memory Verses:
Acts 20:24
2 Corinthians 4:7-10

**WEEK 47**
Colossians 1-2
Colossians 3-4
Ephesians 1-2
Ephesians 3-4
Ephesians 5-6

Memory Verses:
Ephesians 2:8-10
Colossians 2:6-7

**WEEK 48**
Philippians 1-2
Philippians 3-4
Hebrews 1-2
Hebrews 3-4
Hebrews 5-6

Memory Verses:
Philippians 3:7-8
Hebrews 4:14-16

**WEEK 49**
Hebrews 7
Hebrews 8-9
Hebrews 10
Hebrews 11
Hebrews 12

Memory Verses:
Galatians 2:19-20
2 Corinthians 5:17

**WEEK 50**
1 Timothy 1-3
1 Timothy 4-6
2 Timothy 1-2
2 Timothy 3-4
1 Peter 1-2

Memory Verses:
2 Timothy 2:1-2
2 Timothy 2:15

**WEEK 51**
1 Peter 3-4
1 Peter 5, 2 Peter 1
2 Peter 2-3
1 John 1-3
1 John 4-5

Memory Verses:
1 Peter 2:11
1 John 4:10-11

**WEEK 52**
Revelation 1
Revelation 2-3
Revelation 4-5
Revelation 18-19
Revelation 20-22

Memory Verses:
Revelation 3:19
Revelation 21:3-4

# Notes

1. Donald S. Whitney, *Spiritual Disciplines for the Christian Life* (Carol Stream, IL: NavPress, 2014).

2. This story is found in an article in *The Bible Society Journal*, vol. 59, no. 5, May 1913. Article is entitled "A Modern Miracle among the Blind"; https://books.google.com/books?id=KqpVAAAAYAAJ&pg=RA2-PA69&lpg=RA2-PA69&dq=william+mcPherson+tongue+bible+1913&source=bl&ots=uXLe8pfppT&sig=XPVYfSFo80cX7WkziXK7uumpyes&hl=en&sa=X&ved=0ahUKEwjqh5ri0brbAhXN0VMKHdcSDWkQ6AEIOzAD#v=onepage&q=william%20mcPherson%20tongue%20bible%201913&f=false

3. Kay Warren, *Sacred Privilege* (Grand Rapids, MI: Revell, 2017), 164.

4. Julie Manning, *My Heart* (Nashville, TN: B&H Publishing Group, 2017), 159.

5. Joan Horbiak, *50 Ways to Lose Ten Pounds* (Lincolnwood, IL; Publications International, 1995), 95. Although this saying circulated years before, it was attributed to Saint-Exupéry around 2007.

6. Warren, *Sacred Privilege*.

7. Emily Perl Kingsley, *Welcome to Holland* (American Essay, 1987).

8. http://ourrabbijesus.com/articles/does-god-forget-sins/

9. Ibid.

10. https://www.lifeway.com/kidsministry/2017/07/19/nothing-less-than-the-whole-bible/

11. Leroy Eims, *The Lost Art of Disciplemaking* (Grand Rapids, MI: Revell, 1978), 53.

12. https://www.lifeway.com/kidsministry/2017/07/19/nothing-less-than-the-whole-bible/

13. Manning, *My Heart*, 52.

14. Al Mohler, "The Shack—The Missing Art of Evangelical Discernment" (AlbertMohler.com, 2010).

15. "No Man Is an Island" by Tenth Avenue North. Words and Music by Brendon Shirley, Jason Jamison, Jeff Owen, Mike Donehey, and Ruben Juarez.

16. Chrystie Cole, "Biblical Femininity" (Ambassador International, 2013), 21–22.

17. https://jdgreear.com/blog/the-best-of-jen-wilkin/

# Disciplemaking resources to grow your people.

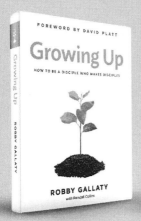

"An outstanding introduction to the basics of the faith in a manner that will equip Christians to grow into maturity."

**THOM S. RAINER**

"I want to encourage you as clearly as I possibly can. Please don't read this book. Instead, do it."

**DAVID PLATT**

"Read this book, be encouraged, and then pass it on to a fellow pilgrim."

**RUSSELL D. MOORE**